POETRY
THEN AND NOW

APPROACHES TO PRE-TWENTIETH CENTURY POETRY

Sheila Hales

Heinemann Educational Publishers
Halley Court, Jordan Hill, Oxford OX2 8EJ
a division of Reed Educational & Professional Publishing Ltd

Oxford   Melbourne   Auckland
Johannesburg   Blantyre   Gaborone
Ibadan   Portsmouth (NH) USA   Chicago

© Sheila Hales 1994

02 01 00 99
10 9 8

ISBN 0 435 14043 4

British Library Cataloguing in Publication Data for this title is available on request

Cover and book design by Moondisks Ltd, Cambridge
Printed and bound by The Bath Press, Bath

Acknowledgements

The authors and publishers would like to thank the following for permission to reproduce copyright material:
Carcanet Press Ltd for 'Overheard in County Sligo' from *Collected Poems* by Gillian Clarke; Wendy Cope for 'Ever So Cute' by Wendy Cope; Jan Dean for 'Writing' by Jan Dean; Faber & Faber Ltd for 'Moon-transport' by Ted Hughes; Greenwillow Press, a division of William Morrow and Company, Inc. for 'The Dragon of Death' from *Nightmares* by Jack Prelutsky © 1976 Jack Prelutsky; Hamish Hamilton for 'Song of the Sea and People' by James Berry from *When I Dance* copyright © James Berry 1988. First published by Hamish Hamilton Children's Books; David Higham Associates Ltd for 'Death of an Aircraft' by Charles Causley; Hippopotamus Press for 'Prince Kano' by Edward Lowbury; James MacGibbon (Executor) for 'Fafnir and the Knights' by Stevie Smith from *The Collected Poems of Stevie Smith* published in Penguin Twentieth-century Classics; McGraw-Hill Book Company for 'The Sun and the Moon' by Elaine Daron from *Free to be...You and Me* published by McGraw Hill Book Company Ltd, New York; Gerda Mayer for 'The Crunch' by Gerda Mayer from *The Candy-Floss Tree* 1984; John Murray for 'Daddy Fell into the Pond' by Alfred Noyes; Judith Nicholls for 'Moonscape' © Judith Nicholls 1985 from *Magic Mirror* by Judith Nicholls published by Faber and Faber; Sean O'Huigin for 'Atmosfear' by Sean O' Huigin from *Learning Through Imagined Experience* published by Hodder and Stoughton Ltd; Penguin Books Ltd for 'In a Far Land', To be a Ghost'; and 'The Closed School' from *To Be A Ghost* by Raymond Wilson copyright © Raymond Wilson 1991 published by Viking; Peters Fraser & Dunlop Group Ltd for 'He who owns the Whistle, rules the World' by Roger McGough from *In the Glassroom* published by Jonathan Cape; Polygon for 'The Choosing' by Liz Lochhead from *Dreaming Frankenstein and Collected Poems* by Liz Lochhead; Rogers Coleridge and White Ltd for 'Winter' by Gareth Owen from *Salford Road and other Poems* © Gareth Owen 1988 by Young Lions and for 'The Lesson' by Edward Lucie-Smith from *A Tropical Childhood and Other Poems* Oxford University Press 1961; George Sassoon for 'In the Pink' and 'In an Underground Dressing Station' by Siegfried Sassoon; Virago for 'Woman Work' by Maya Angelou.

Photos:
p105 Peter Newark's Pictures; p110ff (Woman spinning/Women carrying coal) The Mansell Collection.

Every effort has been made to trace copyright holders of poems in this book but it has not always been possible. We would be glad to rectify any omissions in subsequent printings if notice is given to the publisher.

Contents

Introduction

The poems in this book have been chosen because they have been received enthusiastically by students in Key Stage 3. I began with a huge mountain of pre-twentieth and twentieth century poetry and trialled both the poems and the approaches in Key Stage 3 classrooms. If they didn't work, they were rejected! What we have here are poems which Key Stage 3 students genuinely enjoyed.

The approaches I have suggested emphasize oral work, paired and group readings and group discussions and explorations.

The National Curriculum

This book will meet your needs for poetry at Key Stage 3 for all three attainment targets:

- For **Reading** it includes a wide range of the twentieth century poets and pre-twentieth century poets recommended in the National Curriculum, features a range of forms and includes poets from different cultures and traditions.
- For **Writing** the activities encourage students to learn about a variety of forms, develop their use of poetic devices and write poetry closely related to the poems they read and also poetry based on their own experience.
- For **Speaking and Listening** the activities offer many varied opportunities for reading, presentations and discussion.

Organization

The poems are organized in thematic sections because reading poems on similar themes alongside each other helps to stimulate discussion and debate. The sections often contain a mixture of contemporary and older poems which complement each other.

In the activities, **Looking Closely** sections help students to get to grips with the poems, often working in pairs or groups. In the **Response** sections students are encouraged to produce their own poems, pieces of writing and oral presentations. **Comparing Poems** sections offer specific opportunities for comparison.

The **Drama** section at the end of the book offers extended drama activities for certain poems.

Differentiation

The chapters are arranged broadly in ascending order of difficulty so that easier units are grouped in the first half of the book and more difficult units in the second. In doing so I have looked at the balance of difficulty in a unit overall in terms of accessibility of the language level, sophistication of the theme and demands of the activities. This will help you to use this book as a resource throughout Years 7, 8 and 9.

SHEILA HALES

1 A Twist in the Tale

The four poems in this unit all have unexpected endings. 'Prince Kano' and 'Miller's End' are both by poets from this century. Charles Causley is a very well-known poet who has written poetry for both children and adults. Charles Kingsley and Thomas Haynes Bayly were both writing during the Victorian period.

The Mistletoe Bough

The mistletoe hung in the castle hall,
The holly branch shone on the old oak wall;
And the baron's retainers were blithe and gay,
And keeping their Christmas holiday.
The baron beheld with a father's pride
His beautiful child, young Lovell's bride;
While she with her bright eyes seem'd to be
The star of the goodly company.

'I'm weary of dancing now;' she cried;
'Here tarry a moment – I'll hide – I'll hide!
And, Lovell, be sure thou'rt* first to trace
The clue to my secret lurking place.'
Away she ran – and her friends began
Each tower to search, and each nook to scan;
And young Lovell cried, 'Oh where dost thou hide?
I'm lonesome without thee, my own dear bride.'

● ● ● ● ● ● ● ● ● ● ● ●

They sought her that night! and they sought her next day!
And they sought her in vain when a week pass'd away!
In the highest – the lowest – the loneliest spot,
Young Lovell sought wildly – but found her not.
And years flew by, and their grief at last
Was told as a sorrowful tale long past;
And when Lovell appeared, the children cried,
'See! the old man weeps for his fairy bride.'

At length an oak chest, that had long lain hid,
Was found in the castle – they raised the lid –
And a skeleton form lay mouldering there,
In the bridal wreath of that lady fair!
Oh! sad was her fate! – in sportive jest
She hid from her lord in the old oak chest.
It closed with a spring! – and, dreadful doom,
The bride lay clasp'd in her living tomb!

THOMAS HAYNES BAYLY (1797–1839)

* you are

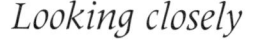

Looking closely

1 Work with a partner.
   a Pick out some of the words in the poem that seem old-fashioned.
   b Now replace these words with a modern equivalent.
   c Does this word change make any difference to the mood of the poem?

2 Work in groups
   a Choose one person to play the part of Lovell.
   b The rest of the group should take turns to question Lovell about the events of that Christmas-time, and of what happened in the years that followed the disappearance of the baron's daughter.

The person playing the part of Lovell should feel free to make up answers, but keep within the story-line of the poem.

● ● ● ● ● ● ● ● ● ● ●

The Sands of Dee

'O Mary, go and call the cattle home,
And call the cattle home,
And call the cattle home,
Across the sands of Dee!'
The western wind was wild and dank with foam,
And all alone went she.

The western tide crept up along the sand,
And o'er and o'er the sand,
And round and round the sand,
As far as eye could see.
The rolling mist came down and hid the land:
And never home came she.

'Oh! is it weed, or fish, or floating hair –
A tress of golden hair,
A drowned maiden's hair,
Above the nets at sea?
Was never salmon yet that shone so fair
Among the stakes on Dee.'

They rowed her in across the rolling foam,
The cruel crawling foam,
The cruel hungry foam,
To her grave beside the sea:
But still the boatmen hear her call the cattle home
Across the sands of Dee

CHARLES KINGSLEY (1819–1875)

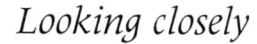

Looking closely

1 Prepare 'The Sands of Dee' for reading aloud. Remember there is a twist in the tale and think about how you are going to build up to the final lines.

   a Try several different ways of reading the poem. Which parts need to be read softly or loudly, slowly or quickly? Where do you need to pause? Which words do you need to stress?

   b Find the places where the poet repeats certain words and phrases. Why do you think he does this? What effect does it have when youare reading the poem aloud?

   c When the same sound is repeated at the beginning of words it is called **alliteration**. One example of alliteration in the poem is 'western wind was wild'. Find other examples of alliteration. What effect does alliteration have when you read the poem aloud?

Response

1 Decide who is speaking in the poem; perhaps more than one person. Imagine you are the speaker in the poem and write about the events of that wild, misty night as you saw them happen. You may decide to write from two different points of view, if you think there are two voices in the poem.

Miller's End

When we moved to Miller's End,
Every afternoon at four
A thin shadow of a shade
Quavered through the garden-door.

Dressed in black from top to toe
And a veil about her head
To us all it seemed as though
She came walking from the dead.

With a basket on her arm
Through the hedge-gap she would pass,
Never a mark that we could spy
On the flagstones or the grass.

When we told the garden-boy
How we saw the phantom glide,
With a grin his face was bright
As the pool he stood beside.

'That's no ghost-walk,' Billy said,
'Nor a ghost you fear to stop –
Only old Miss Wickerby
On a short cut to the shop.'

So next day we lay in wait,
Passed a civil time of day,
Said how pleased we were she came
Daily down our garden-way.

Suddenly her cheek it paled,
Turned, as quick, from ice to flame.
'Tell me,' said Miss Wickerby.
'Who spoke of me, and my name?'

'Bill the garden-boy.'
She sighed,
Said, 'Of course, you could not know
How he drowned – that very pool –
A frozen winter – long ago.'

CHARLES CAUSLEY (1917–   )

● ● ● ● ● ● ● ● ● ● ● ●

Looking closely

1   In the first three verses of this poem Charles Causley has chosen to use words and phrases that create a chilling atmosphere.

    a   Write down any words or word clusters that convinced you that Miss Wickerby was a ghost.

    b   When did you suspect that Billy was a ghost – at the end of the poem, or was there a moment earlier in the poem? Share your response with others in the class.

2   Discuss the title of the poem. What was Miller's End? How do 'Miller' and 'End' connect with the whole poem?

Response

1   Write the story that is told in 'Miller's End' as a radio play. You will need at least four characters, one of whom could also act as a narrator. Include directions for sound effects (FX), and set out your script clearly.

Example

FX	Opening music from …
	Sound of rushing water to run under:
Gemma:	Welcome to our new home. Pretty spot, isn't it? The pool, the river, ducks and nesting moorhens. I'm Gemma, and this is my younger brother …
David:	(interrupting) I can speak for myself, thanks!

When you have written your scripts choose some to record in groups.

Prince Kano

In a dark wood Prince Kano, lost his way
And searched in vain through the long summer's day.
At last, when night was near, he came in sight
Of a small clearing filled with yellow light,
And there, bending beside his brazier, stood
A charcoal burner wearing a black hood.
The Prince cried out for joy: 'Good friend, I'll give
What you will ask: guide me to where I live.'
The man pulled back his hood: he had no face –
Where it should be there was an empty space.
Half dead with fear the Prince staggered away,
Rushed blindly through the wood till break of day;
And then he saw a larger clearing, filled
With houses, people; but his soul was chilled,
He looked around for comfort, and his search
Led him inside a small, half-empty church
Where monks prayed. 'Father,' to one he said,
'I've seen a dreadful thing; I am afraid.'
'What did you see, my son?' 'I saw a man
Whose face was like…' and, as the Prince began,
The monk drew back his hood and seemed to hiss
Pointing to where his face should be, 'Like this?'

EDWARD LOWBURY (1913–   )

16

Looking closely

1 Discuss your first impressions of the poem:
   - Were you expecting the ending?
   - Did you find the poem frightening, chilling or mysterious? Why?
   - What was Prince Kano hoping to find when he saw the houses, the people, the church and the monk?
   - Why is it particularly chilling when the monk turns out to be a faceless man?

Comparing poems

1 a In groups discuss which poem you think has the most startling ending.
   b Imagine you are a panel of experts about to award the Twist in the Tale Poetry Prize for the best poem of the year. From the thousands of entrants, a short-list of these four poems has been drawn up.
   c Prepare the speech you will give at the award ceremony. In it you should mention the merits of each poem, before announcing the winner and saying why you have chosen that one.

2 Gothic Poetry

During the late eighteenth and early nineteenth centuries gothic stories and poems became very popular. Gothic stories were usually set in medieval times in strange and mysterious places. People loved to read stories and poems set in bleak towers and castles, haunted by the ghosts of sinister monks and languishing ladies. 'The Eve of St Agnes' by John Keats is a typically Gothic poem. It is a long poem, so only part of it has been reprinted here.

The Eve of St Agnes (extract)

This narrative poem is set in a huge, lonely house which stands on a windswept moor. Porphyro and Madeline are in love, but Madeline's rich, powerful relatives are determined to keep the lovers apart.

20 January, the Eve of St Agnes, is traditionally the time when young girls may dream of their future love. As Madeline prepares to go to bed on this special night, Porphyro has persuaded an old woman to lead him to Madeline's room.

> He follow'd through a lowly arched way
> Brushing the cobwebs with his lofty plume,
> And as she mutter'd 'Well-a … well-a-day!'
> He found him in a little moonlight room,
> Pale, lattic'd, chill, and silent as a tomb.

Madeline, hoping for no more than a vision of her lover, finds him actually in the room. Together, they plan to run away.

Down the wide stairs a darkling way they found. –
In all the house was heard no human sound.
A chain-droop'd lamp was flickering by each door;
The arras*, rich with horseman, hawk, and hound,
Flutter'd in the besieging wind's uproar;
And the long carpets rose along the gusty floor.

They glide, like phantoms, into the wide hall;
Like phantoms, to the iron porch, they glide;
Where lay the Porter, in uneasy sprawl,
With a huge empty flaggon by his side:
The wakeful bloodhound rose, and shook his hide,
But his sagacious eye an inmate owns:
By one, and one, the bolts full easy slide: –
The chains lie silent on the footworn stones; –
The key turns, and the door upon its hinges groans.

And they are gone: aye, ages long ago
These lovers fled away into the storm.

JOHN KEATS (1795–1821)

* tapestry

Looking closely

1 It was not only gothic literature which became fashionable two
   hundred years ago, but also gothic buildings and landscapes. Ruins
   of abbeys and towers were much admired, so much so that wealthy
   people even built 'ruins' in the grounds of their homes! Mock castles
   sprang up all over England, complete with long, dark halls, ornate,
   gloomy furniture, and arched doorways. Think of Count Dracula in
   his castle and there you have the perfect gothic setting. Keeping this
   in mind, pick out all the words that Keats has used to create a gothic
   setting for his poem.

2 Draw a plan of the route the lovers used to escape from the house.
   On your plan, label all the significant features of the house, together
   with the potentially dangerous obstacles they had to pass. Use the
   words from the poem to help you with your labelling.

In A Far Land

In a far land
a black mountain broods:
beneath the black mountain
stretch the green woods.

Among the green woods
a white castle soars:
in the white castle
are dark corridors.

The corridors lead
to a black, shut door.
Behind it a Prince
sprawls dead on the floor.

With a cobwebbed cup
by his withered hand,
a Prince lies poisoned
in that far land.

A hobbling old Princess
creeps to that door –
ghost calling ghost
for evermore!

She murmurs her guilt
in sighs and soft moans.
Behind the locked door
the dead Prince groans.

RAYMOND WILSON (1925–   )

Looking closely

1 When you read the poem, did you notice how one verse lead easily
into the next? It's rather like the stories for young children which
begin, 'In a dark, dark town there's a dark, dark street.'

   a Rewrite the first three verses in that format, for example:
     'In a far, far land…

   b Discuss which words you needed to keep, and which you could
     discard.

Response

1 Write your own ghostly poem using the same format, with one verse
leading into the next. In each brief verse, you should describe the
next gothic setting of the journey. What will be your final
destination, and what will you find when you arrive there, a
poisoned prince, or something far more frightening?

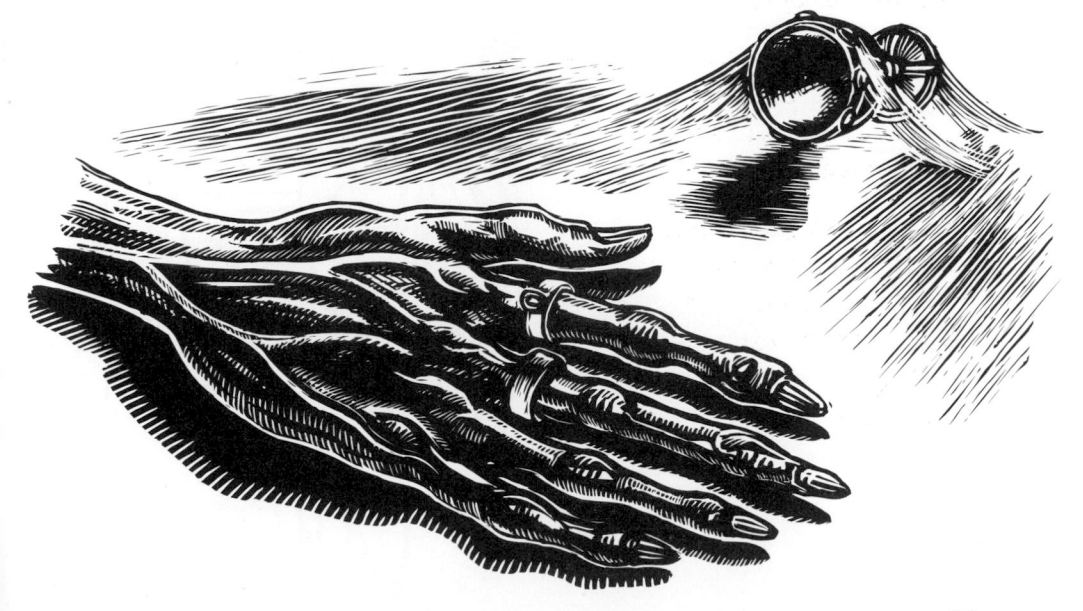

To be a Ghost

To be a ghost
it helps if you're able
to moan pitifully
like the night wind
in the tormented wood,
and can whine in chimneys,
wail down corridors,
bump and thump about
and rattle chains
in distant dungeons.

To be a ghost
it helps to have
a mouldering churchyard,
a monk's robes and hood
and a grinning skull,
dark shadows of yew trees
and a ruined abbey
with screech-owls flitting
through spectral moonlight
as midnight chimes.

These are the stock-in-trade
the public demands,
without which no claim
to be a ghost
can be considered serious.

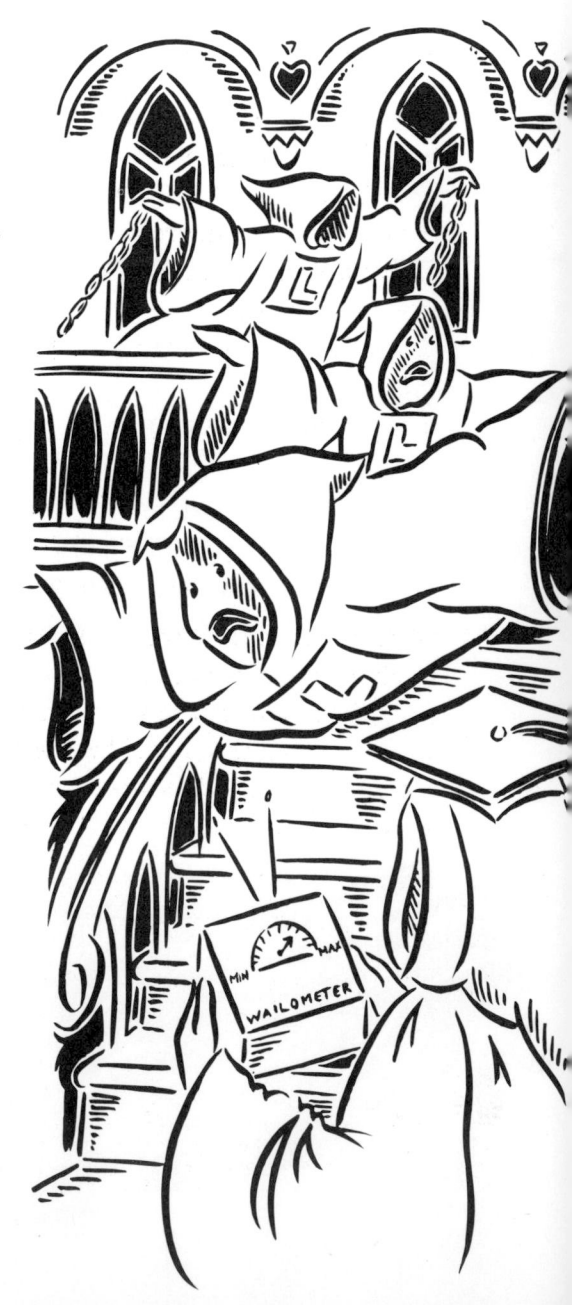

But truly to be a ghost
what you need is
to be locked without hope of escape
in a time and place
and suffering
that not even centuries
can change; and of course
you must be dead.
But you mustn't know it!

RAYMOND WILSON (1925–   )

Response

1   Write a 'Guide For Ghosts'. This is a handbook which would be given
to all new ghosts to explain what is expected of them. Use the ideas
from the poem to help you write the Guide. Think about the best
way to set out this guide, for example, what sub-headings would
you use? You could include illustrations or diagrams to help your
explanations.

The Closed School

Under the silvering light of the cold, tall sky,
Where the stars are like glimmering ice and the moon
   rides high,
Bolted and locked since the war by long-dead hands,
Next to the shadowy church, the closed school stands.

A village school, in the grip of frost and the past,
Its classrooms airless as tombs, its corridors waste;
Behind boarded windows barely an insect crawls
On the spreading atlas that is staining ceiling and
   walls.

Here is the stillness of death. Listen hard as you can,
There's not one sound to be heard that is noisier than
The creeping of mould, or the crumbling of masonry
Into a fine floor-dust, soft and powdery.

Only deeper than silence, at the far end of listening,
Come the feet in the corridors, silver voices that ring
In the raftered hall, and outside, where the frost freezes hard,
Brittle laughter of children snowballing in the yard.

RAYMOND WILSON (1925–   )

Response

1 This poem sends a shiver down my spine because I do not usually think of a school as a ghostly place.

    a Think about other places which are not usually associated with the supernatural – perhaps a fire station, or a bank, or a park.

    b Write a ghostly description of your chosen place. Select your words very carefully to create the right atmosphere.

● ● ● ● ● ● ● ● ● ● ● ●

The Witch

I have walked a great while over the snow,
And I am not tall nor strong.
My clothes are wet, and my teeth are set,
And the way was hard and long.
I have wandered over the fruitful earth,
But I never came here before.
Oh, lift me over the threshold, and let me in at the door!

The cutting wind is a cruel foe.
I dare not stand in the blast.
My hands are stone, and my voice a groan,
And the worst of death is past.
I am but a little maiden still,
My little white feet are sore.
Oh, lift me over the threshold, and let me in at the door!

Her voice was the voice that women have,
Who plead for their heart's desire.
She came – she came – and the quivering flame
Sank and died in the fire.
It never was lit again on my hearth
Since I hurried across the floor.
To lift her over the threshold, and let her in at the door.

MARY COLERIDGE (1861–1907)

(see Drama Approaches page 151)

Looking closely

1 Work with a partner to prepare this poem for reading aloud. It is a
   very strange, mysterious poem and you will have to decide what it
   means to you before you can perform it.

   a First write out the poem quickly, to give yourself a working copy to
      make notes on.

   b Now read the poem again. Think about the mood of the poem:
      ● Is it serious, frightening, moving or solemn?
      ● Does the mood change? If so, where does it change and how?

   c Think about the voice of the poem:
      ● Who is speaking?
      ● Where does the voice change to someone different?

Mark these changes on your copy. You may decide to change readers to
show where the mood or voice has changed.

   d Now discuss the two voices in more detail:

   First Voice
      ● Who is the girl?
      ● What does she want? What is her real motive in asking to be let in?
      ● When the girl says 'my hands are stone' what does she mean?
      ● When she says 'the worst of death is past' what do you think
         she really means?

   Second Voice
      ● Who is the second person?
      ● How does this person feel when she/he hears the girl's voice?
      ● How does this person feel at the end of the poem?
      ● How can you use your voice to show any change of feelings, for
         example, from anxiety to fear?

   e Look at the whole poem again. Put a mark by any words you feel
      need special treatment, such as 'S' for softly or 'M' for with menace.

   f When you and your partner are satisfied with your reading,
      perform the poem for another pair in the class. Compare your
      reading with other readings.

3 Poems to Make You Smile

Poetry can be thought-provoking, challenging, moving or dramatic.
A poem can also be written simply as a piece of entertainment. Here
are four poems to make you smile. William Walsh wrote his poem
about three hundred years ago, and Robert Southey was writing about
two hundred years ago, but both poems still make us smile today!

The Despairing Lover

Distracted with care
For Phyllis the fair,
Since nothing could move her,
Poor Damon, her lover,
Resolves in despair
No longer to languish,
Nor bear so much anguish:
But, mad with his love,
To a precipice goes,
Where a leap from above
Would soon finish his woes.

When in rage he came there,
Beholding how steep
The sides did appear,
And the bottom how deep;
His torments projecting,
And sadly reflecting,

That a lover forsaken
A new love may get,
But a neck, when once broken,
Can never be set:
And, that he could die
Whenever he would,
But, that he could live
But as long as he could:
How grievous soever
The torment might grow,
He scorn'd to endeavour
To finish it so.
But bold, unconcern'd
At thoughts of the pain,
He calmly return'd
To his cottage again.

WILLIAM WALSH (1663–1708)

● ● ● ● ● ● ● ● ● ● ● ●

Looking closely

1 The rhythm and pace of this poem are very important; each short
   line seems to hurry the poem forward, carrying the reader up to that
   precipice, and then quickly home with Damon to the cottage.
   First, try reading the poem slowly. Now read the poem a second
   time; this time read quite quickly, only slowing the pace in the last
   four lines.
   ● Which reading of the poem did you prefer?
   ● Which reading helped you to make more sense of the poem?

2 a William Walsh seems to have a great deal of sympathetic under-
     standing for Damon. What do you think of Damon? Talk with
     others about the kind of man you imagine him to have been:
     ● Was he rich or poor?
     ● What was his job?
     ● How do you think he met Phyllis?
     ● How did Phyllis feel about him?
     ● Was Damon a particularly romantic character?
     ● How may he have spent the rest of his life after his return to
       the cottage?

   b Use the ideas from your discussion to write an obituary for
     Damon. You will have to decide how and when he eventually
     died.

The King of the Crocodiles

'Now, woman, why without your veil?
And wherefore do you look so pale?
And, woman, why do you groan so sadly,
And wherefore beat your bosom madly?'

'Oh, I have lost my darling child,
And that's the loss that makes me wild;
He stoop'd by the river down to drink,
And there was a Crocodile by the brink.

He did not venture in to swim,
He only stoop'd to drink at the brim;
But under the reeds the Crocodile lay,
And struck with his tail and swept him away.

Now take me in your boat, I pray,
For down the river lies my way,
And me to the Reed Island bring,
For I will go to the Crocodile King.

And to the King I will complain
How my poor child was wickedly slain;
The King of Crocodiles he is good,
And I shall have the murderer's blood.'

The man replied, 'No, woman, no;
To the Island of Reeds I will not go;
I would not for any worldly thing
See the face of the Crocodile King.'

'Then lend me now your little boat,
And I will down the river float,
I tell thee that no worldly thing
Shall keep me from the Crocodile King.'

The woman she leapt into the boat,
And down the river alone did she float,
And fast with the stream the boat proceeds,
And now she is come to the Island of Reeds.

The King of the Crocodiles there was seen;
He sat upon the eggs of the Queen,
And all around, a numerous rout,
The young Prince Crocodiles crawl'd about.

She fell upon her bended knee,
And said, 'O King, have pity on me,
For I have lost my darling child,
And that's the loss that makes me wild.

A crocodile ate him for his food:
Now let me have the murderer's blood;
Let me have vengeance for my boy,
The only thing that can give me joy.

I know that you, sire, never do wrong,
You have no tail so stiff and strong,
You have no tail to strike and slay,
But you have ears to hear what I say.'

'You have done well,' the king replies,
And fix'd on her his little eyes;
'Good woman, yes, you have done right;
But you have not described me quite.

I have no tail to strike and slay,
And I have ears to hear what you say;
I have teeth, moreover, as you may see,
And I will make a meal of thee.'

'A meal of me!' the woman cried,
Taking wit in her anger, and courage beside;
She took him his forelegs and hind between
And trundled him off the eggs of the Queen.

Two Crocodile Princes, as they played on the sand,
She caught, and grasping them one in each hand,
Thrust the head of one into the throat of the other,
And made each Prince crocodile choke his brother.

And when she had trussed three couple this way,
She carried them off and hastened away,
And plying her oars with might and main,
Crossed the river and got to the shore again.

When the Crocodile queen came home, she found
That her eggs were broken and scattered around,
And that six young princes, darlings all,
Were missing; for none of them answered her call.

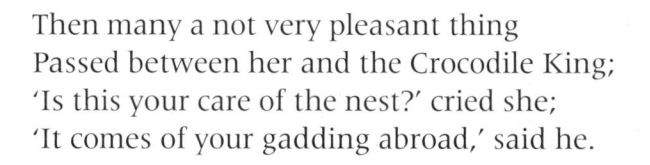

Then many a not very pleasant thing
Passed between her and the Crocodile King;
'Is this your care of the nest?' cried she;
'It comes of your gadding abroad,' said he.

The Queen had the better in this dispute,
And the Crocodile King found it best to be mute;
While a terrible peal in his ears she rung,
For the Queen had a tail as well as a tongue.

The woman, meantime, was very well pleased,
She had saved her life, and her heart was eased;
The justice she asked in vain for her son,
She had taken herself, and six for one.

'Mash–Allah!' her neighbours exclaimed in delight,
She gave them a funeral supper that night,
Where they all agreed that revenge was sweet,
And young Prince Crocodiles delicate meat.

ROBERT SOUTHEY (1795–1821)

● ● ● ● ● ● ● ● ● ● ● ●

Response

1 You are going to tell the story as:
    a a sad and tragic event
    b a joke.

Before you begin:

- Briefly write out the main points from the poem which you can work from each time.
- Decide which points you need to emphasize, and which points you will just mention or play down.

Example

Main point: *the woman's son was eaten by a crocodile*

    a Tragic tale: Describe this terrible event in detail, include the woman's feelings.
    b Joke: Mention this part in passing.

- Decide on your tone of voice. For example, you will need to sound very sad in parts of the tragic tale, even dropping your voice to a horrified whisper.
- Think about your choice of vocabulary.

Example

Whoops! There go his legs is fine for a joke, but hardly appropriate for a sad and tragic event.

2 'The King of the Crocodiles' is written in rhyming couplets, that is, pairs of lines which rhyme throughout the poem. Try writing in this style. Write about what happened in the poem from the point of view of the Crocodile King.

You could start like this:

A woman came to me one day
To grovel in a sickening way...

Daddy Fell into the Pond

Everyone grumbled. The sky was grey.
We had nothing to do and nothing to say.
We were nearing the end of a dismal day.
And there seemed to be nothing beyond,
   Then
      Daddy fell into the pond!

And everyone's face grew merry and bright,
And Timothy danced for sheer delight.
'Give me the camera, quick, oh quick!
He's crawling out of the duckweed!' Click!

Then the gardener suddenly slapped his knee,
And doubled up, shaking silently,
And the ducks all quacked as if they were daft,
And it sounded as if the old drake laughed.
Oh, there wasn't a thing that didn't respond
   When
      Daddy fell into the pond!

ALFRED NOYES (1880–1959)

The Crunch

The lion and his tamer
They had a little tiff,
For the lion limped too lamely, –
The bars had bored him stiff.

No call to crack your whip, Sir!
Said the lion then irate:
No need to snap my head off,
Said the tamer – but too late.

GERDA MAYER (1927–   )

Response

1 Work in groups to write your own humorous nonsense poem.
   a Begin with one of these first lines:
   - We set off to sea on a Summer's day...
   - The old man and his cat...
   - The parrot, the dog and the kangaroo...

   b Alternatively, choose a line of your own. Write the line at the top
      of a piece of paper. Pass the paper round the group. Everyone
      should add one line of the poem. Keep going until you think you
      have reached a funny punch line.

4 Dragon Days

Dragons have featured in poetry since the first early poems and legends were written down, well over 1,000 years ago. The poems in this unit show different views of dragons over the centuries. When Samuel Rowlands was writing during the reign of Elizabeth 1 some people would still have believed that dragons really existed. By the time Tennyson wrote 'The Kraken' last century people would have known that dragons only appear in myths and legends. However, dragons continue to play an important part in our imagination as the final poem in this unit shows.

Sir Eglamour

Sir Eglamour, that worthy knight,
He took his sword and went to fight:
And as he rode both hill and dale,
Armed upon his shirt of mail,
A dragon came out of his den,
Had slain, God knows how many men!

When he espied Sir Eglamour,
Oh, if you had but heard him roar,
And seen how all the trees did shake,
The knight did tremble, horse did quake,
The birds betake them all to peeping –
It would have made you fall a weeping!

But now it is in vain to fear,
Being come unto, 'fight dog! fight bear!'
To it they go and fiercely fight
A live-long day from morn till night.
The dragon had a plaguy hide,
And could the sharpest steel abide.

No sword will enter him with cuts,
Which vexed the knight unto the guts:
But, as in choler he did burn,
He watched the dragon a good turn;
And, as a yawning he did fall,
He thrust his sword in, hilts and all.

Then, like a coward, he to fly
Unto his den that was hard by;
And there he lay all night and roared.
The knight was sorry for his sword,
But, riding thence, said, 'I forsake it,
He that will fetch it, let him take it!'

SAMUEL ROWLANDS (1570–1630)

● ● ● ● ● ● ● ● ● ● ● ●

Looking closely

1 In groups read the poem aloud.

   a Think about the meaning of the poem, and then divide the lines
      between the group. You could bring in a different voice to read
      the lines spoken by Sir Eglamour. Try out different readings.

   b Discuss the tone of voice you are using as you read. For example,
      are your voices happy, triumphant, fearful or sorrowful? Are you
      speaking loudly or softly?

   c How would you describe the mood of the poem?

2 'Sir Eglamour' contains a number of words which you may not
   know. Guess the meaning of the following:
   worthy, espied, quake, betake, in vain, plaguy, hide, abide, vexed,
   choler, hilts, hard by, thence, forsake

Use the context of the poem to help you discover the meanings. If
you're still puzzled, use a good dictionary to look up the meaning of
any words you are unsure of.

Fafnir and the Knights

In the quiet waters
Of the forest pool
Fafnir the dragon
His tongue will cool

His tongue will cool
And his muzzle dip
Until the soft waters lave
His muzzle-tip

Happy the dragon
In the days expended
Before the time had come for dragons
To be hounded

Delivered in their simplicity
To the Knights of the Advancing Band
Who seeing the simple dragon
Must kill him out of hand.

When thy body shall be torn
And thy lofty spirit
Broken into pieces
For a Knight's merit,

When thy life-blood shall be spilt
And thy Being mild
In torment and dismay
To Death beguiled

Fafnir, I shall say then,
Thou art better dead
For the Knights have burnt thy grass
And thou couldst not have fed.

The time has not come yet
But must come soon
Meanwhile happy Fafnir
Take thy rest in the afternoon.

Take thy rest
Fafnir while thou mayest
In the long grass
Where thou liest

Happy knowing not
In thy simplicity
That the Knights have come
To do away with thee.

STEVIE SMITH (1902–1971)

Looking closely

1 Use the following questions to help you to discuss the poem:
   a Why does the poet describe Fafnir as happy? When is the dragon happy?
   b What terrible things do knights do to dragons? Why?
   c What do you think the poet thinks about 'a Knight's merit'?
   d Look at the words used to describe the dragon. What sort of dragon is presented in this poem? Is it a typical view of dragons?
   e Although the poem is a modern day poem the poet has used old-fashioned words such as 'thee' and 'thou'. Why do you think she has done this?

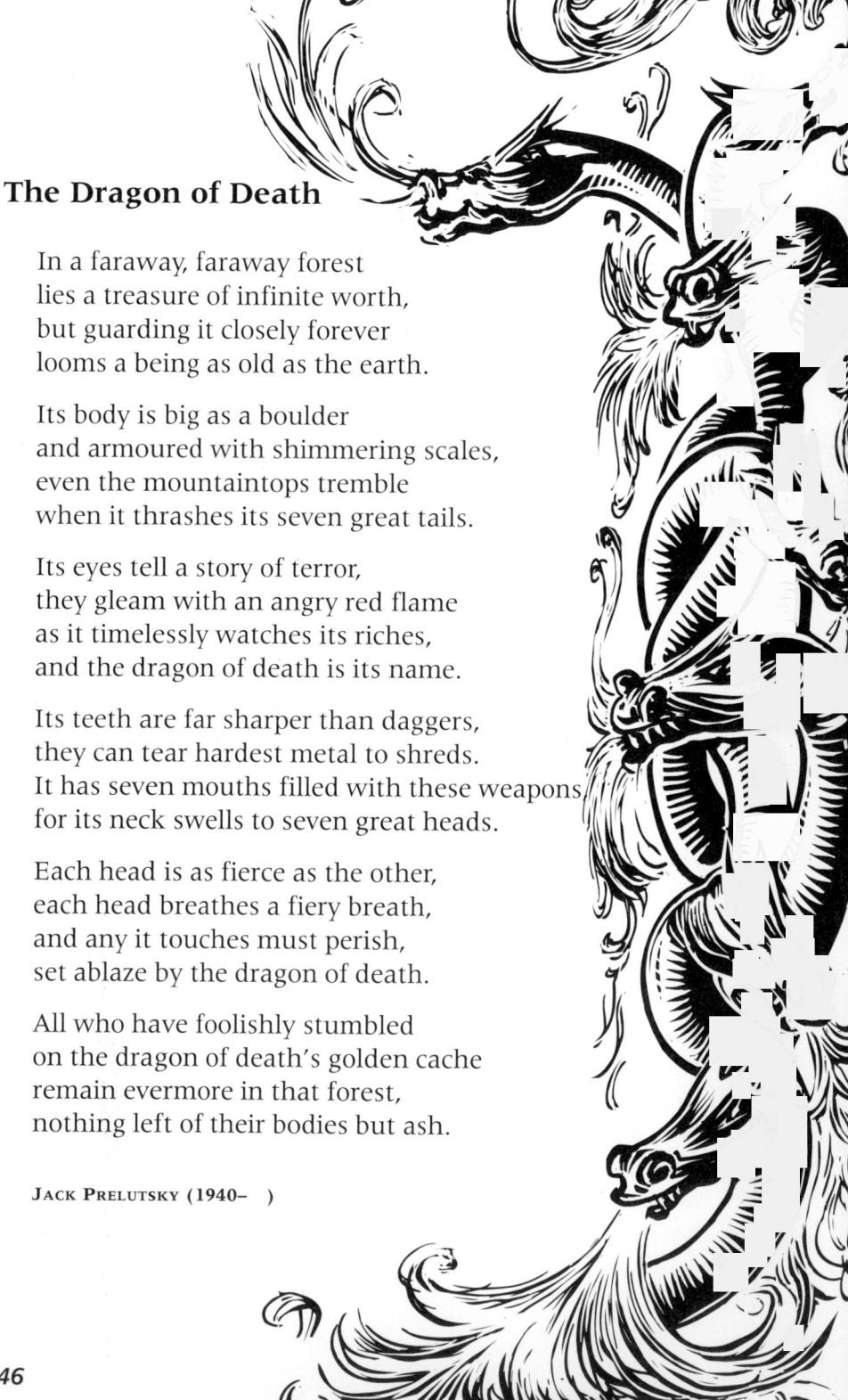

The Dragon of Death

In a faraway, faraway forest
lies a treasure of infinite worth,
but guarding it closely forever
looms a being as old as the earth.

Its body is big as a boulder
and armoured with shimmering scales,
even the mountaintops tremble
when it thrashes its seven great tails.

Its eyes tell a story of terror,
they gleam with an angry red flame
as it timelessly watches its riches,
and the dragon of death is its name.

Its teeth are far sharper than daggers,
they can tear hardest metal to shreds.
It has seven mouths filled with these weapons
for its neck swells to seven great heads.

Each head is as fierce as the other,
each head breathes a fiery breath,
and any it touches must perish,
set ablaze by the dragon of death.

All who have foolishly stumbled
on the dragon of death's golden cache
remain evermore in that forest,
nothing left of their bodies but ash.

JACK PRELUTSKY (1940–)

Comparing poems

1 Draw two outlines of dragons and cut them out.
  In one dragon shape write all the words used to describe the dragon
  in 'Fafnir'. In the other write all the words used to describe the
  dragon in 'The Dragon of Death'.

  In each shape add extra words to describe gentle or fierce dragons.
  Which view of dragons is most typical? Does reading Stevie Smith's
  view of dragons change your view of dragons in any way?

Response

1 Write your own poem about a dragon. Decide what sort of
  personality you want your dragon to have. Will it be fierce or gentle?
  Before you begin look back at the words you wrote down from
  'Fafnir' and 'The Dragon of Death'.

The Kraken

Below the thunders of the upper deep;
Far far beneath in the abysmal sea,
His ancient, dreamless, uninvaded sleep,
The Kraken sleepeth: faintest sunlights flee
About his shadowy sides: above him swell
Huge sponges of millennial growth and height;
And far away into the sickly light,
From many a wondrous grot and secret cell
Unnumber'd and enormous polypi
Winnow with giant fins the slumbering green.
There hath he lain for ages and will lie
Battening upon huge seaworms in his sleep,
Until the latter fire shall heat the deep;
Then once by men and angels to be seen,
In roaring he shall rise and on the surface die.

A L TENNYSON (1809–1902)

● ● ● ● ● ● ● ● ● ● ● ●

Looking closely

1   Discuss your impressions of the Kraken.

Why do you think he will die as soon as he rises to the surface?

Response

1   Draw a picture of the Kraken sleeping in his den under the sea. Use your imagination to decide what he looks like. Look carefully at the descriptions in the poem when you draw his surroundings.

2   What do you think the Kraken really is? Why do you think the Kraken has been sleeping under the sea for years? How do you think he got there?

Write the story of how the Kraken came to be sleeping under the sea more than one thousand years ago.

● ● ● ● ● ● ● ● ● ● ● ●

Atmosfear (extract)

...beneath the drifts
of glittering snow
lies something evil
something low
something with long icy teeth
something curled up
underneath the
ancient glaciers'
mighty cliffs
with blue cold steely
snarling lips
for centuries
it's lain there
trapped inside
its icy lair
listening as
each year goes
past to the
winter's icy
blast
but bit by bit
and drop by drop
as humans make the
air grow hot
pumping garbage
and pollution
they give to it a
neat solution to its
problem of

entrapment
it grinds its jaws
it tries to snap
them

SEAN O'HUIGIN

(see Drama Approaches, page 152)

Looking closely

1 a Look carefully at the spelling of the title. What does the title mean?
  b Look at the way the poem is set out on the page. Why is it so
    long and thin?
  c Read the poem aloud. There is no punctuation, so when you read
    you will have to use your own pauses and emphasis to help the
    meaning come through.

Comparing poems

1 These poems are all about dragons of one kind or another, but each
  poet feels differently about the creature he or she has created. Using
  one or two sentences for each poem, write about each poet's view
  of dragons.

2 If you had to choose just two of these poems to be read together as
  a pair, which two would you choose? Think carefully about why you
  would make your choice. Would you choose two poems that are
  vividly descriptive or two poems with contrasting moods? Explain
  your choice to the rest of the class.

5 The Moon

The moon has long been a favourite subject for writers, particularly poets. P B Shelley was one of a group of poets known as the Romantic poets and, like other romantic poets, he believed that the imagination is extremely powerful.

Leo Tolstoy is probably the best known of all Russian writers. As well as poetry he wrote novels: the most famous are *Anna Karenina* and *War and Peace*.

The Moon

And, like a dying lady lean and pale,
Who totters forth, wrapp'd in a gauzy veil,
Out of her chamber, led by the insane
And feeble wanderings of her fading brain,
The moon arose up in the murky east
A white and shapeless mass.

Art thou pale for weariness
Of climbing heaven and gazing on the earth,
Wandering companionless
Among the stars that have a different birth,
And ever changing, like a joyless eye
That finds no object worth its constancy?

P B SHELLEY (1792–1822)

● ● ● ● ● ● ● ● ● ● ● ●

Looking closely

1 a Write down all the words and phrases from the poem which
could be linked to a woman, for example 'totters' to describe
how she moves.

b Make sure you know *exactly* what your words and phrases mean.
Draw a quick sketch of the woman.

c Now draw a sketch of this particular moon in the night sky. Your
first drawing will obviously influence your second drawing.

d **Personification** is when a writer makes an object or a creature
seem human. Think about the two pictures and try to explain, in
a few short sentences, how Shelley has personified the moon.

Night Airs and Moonshine

Night airs that make tree-shadows walk, and sheep
Washed white in the cold moonshine on grey cliffs.

WALTER SAVAGE LANDOR (1775–1864)

Looking closely

1 a Read these two lines aloud. What pictures came into your head as
  you read? Take turns to describe what you imagined to a partner.
  b Did you notice how sounds are repeated in the poem? Where are
  the 'w', 'sh', and 'c' sounds repeated?
  c Read the poem aloud again. This time, be aware of these
  repeated sounds.

Repeated sounds like this are called **alliteration**.

Response

1 Write down your own two-line poem about a place you know well,
  perhaps lit by moonlight. If you can, include some repeated sounds
  as you write. When you have finished, share your lines with your
  partner.

The Duck and the Moon

A duck was once swimming along the river
looking for fish.
The whole day passed
without her finding a single one.
  When night came
she saw the moon reflected on the water,
and thinking it was a fish
she dived down to catch it.
The other ducks saw her,
and they all made fun of her.
  From that day
the duck was so ashamed and so timid,
that even when she did see a fish under water
she would not try to catch it,
and before long she died of hunger.

LEO TOLSTOY (1828–1910)

Looking closely

1 Talk about these ideas with a partner: If the duck were human:
   - What would the fish be that she was looking for?
   - What would the moon be – something that she could not have?
   - What sort of people would the other ducks be who made fun
     of her?
   - What would have made her feel ashamed and timid?
   - What would have happened to her at the end of the poem? If she
     died, how would she have died?
   Share your ideas with the rest of the class.

The Sun and the Moon

The Sun is filled with shining light,
It blazes far and wide.
The Moon reflects the sunlight back
But has no light inside.

I think I'd rather be the Sun
That shines so bold and bright
Than be the Moon, that only glows
With someone else's light.

ELAINE DARON

Moonscape

No air, no mist, no man, no beast.
No water flows from her Sea of Showers,
no trees, no flowers fringe her Lake of Dreams.
No grass grows or clouds shroud her high hills
or deep deserts. No whale blows in her dry
                        Ocean of Storms.

JUDITH NICHOLLS (1941–   )

Moon-transport

Some people on the moon are so idle
They will not so much as saunter much less sidle.

But if they cannot bear to walk, or try,
How do they get to the places where they lie?

They gather together, as people do for a bus.
'All aboard, whoever's coming with us.'

Then they climb on to each other till they are all
Clinging in one enormous human ball.

Then they roll, and so, without lifting their feet,
Progress quite successfully down the street.

TED HUGHES (1930–   )

Response

1 'Moonscape' could be a negative poem and yet, by listing all the
   things that are not present on the moon, Judith Nicholls has created
   a beautiful image of a sterile world.

Use the same technique to write your own poem about deep space or a
dead star. Write about things which would *not* be there.
What mood are you trying to create by your choice of images? For
example, you could create a very angry poem by writing about no war,
no hate, no guns etc.

2 'Moon Transport' is a lot of fun. Write your own poem about
   something that lives on the moon. Have fun with your poem. You
   can be as over the top as you like – after all, no-one is expected to
   believe you!

If you are stuck for something to write about, try one of these titles:

Cats on the Moon
Moon Balloons
Moon Soup

6 War

Hundreds, perhaps thousands of poems have been written on the subject of war. This is just a small selection. The first poem was written over 150 years ago and the last is a modern poem. Two of the poems were written by Siegfried Sassoon who fought as an officer in the First World War. During battle he was extremely reckless and was nicknamed 'Mad Jack' by the other soldiers. However, he was sickened by what he saw in the trenches and on the battlefield and wrote his poems as a protest against war.

After Blenheim

It was a summer evening,
   Old Kaspar's work was done,
And he before his cottage door
   Was sitting in the sun:
And by him sported on the green
His little grandchild Wilhelmine

She saw her brother Peterkin
   Roll something large and round
Which he beside the rivulet
   In playing there had found:
He came to ask what he had found
That was so large, and smooth, and round.

Old Kaspar took it from the boy
   Who stood expectant by;
And then the old man shook his head,
   And with a natural sigh
''Tis some poor fellow's skull,' said he,
'Who fell in the great victory.

● ● ● ● ● ● ● ● ● ● ●

'I find them in the garden,
   For there's many here about;
And often when I go to plough
   The ploughshare turns them out.
For many thousand men,' said he,
'Were slain in that great victory.'

'Now tell us what 'twas all about,'
   Young Peterkin, he cries;
And little Wilhelmine looks up
   With wonder-waiting eyes;
'Now tell us all about the war,
And what they fought each other for.'

'It was the English,' Kaspar cried,
   Who put the French to rout;
But what they fought each other for
   I could not well make out.
But everybody said,' quoth he,
'That 'twas a famous victory.

'My father lived at Blenheim then,
   Yon little stream hard by;
They burnt his dwelling to the ground,
   And he was forced to fly:
So with his wife and child he fled
Nor had he where to rest his head.

'With fire and sword the country round
   Was wasted far and wide,
And many a childing mother then,
   And newborn baby died:
But things like that, you know, must be
At every famous victory.

● ● ● ● ● ● ● ● ● ● ●

'They say it was a shocking sight
    After the field was won;
For many thousand bodies here
    Lay rotting in the sun:
But things like that, you know, must be
After a famous victory.

'Great praise the Duke of Marlboro' won
    And our good Prince Eugene.'
'Why 'twas a very wicked thing!'
    Said little Wilhelmine;
'Nay…nay…my little girl,' quoth he,
'It was a famous victory.

'And everybody praised the Duke
    Who this great fight did win.'
'But what good came of it at last?'
    Quoth little Peterkin.
'Why that I cannot tell,' said he,
'But 'twas a famous victory.'

ROBERT SOUTHEY (1774–1834)

Looking closely

1 How many people are speaking in the poem? Who are they?

2 The little girl says the battle was 'a very wicked thing'. The old man says 'twas a famous victory'. What do you think?

● ● ● ● ● ● ● ● ● ● ● ●

Horses Aboard

Horses in horsecloths stand in a row
On board the huge ship that at last lets go:
Whither are they sailing? They do not know,
Nor what for, nor how. –
                          They are horses of war,
And are going to where there is fighting afar;
But they gaze through their eye-holes unwitting they are,
And that in some wilderness, gaunt and ghast,
Their bones will bleach ere a year has passed,
And the item be as 'war-waste' classed.–
And when the band booms, and the folk say 'Good-bye!'
And the shore slides astern, they appear wrenched awry
From the scheme Nature planned for them – wondering why.

THOMAS HARDY (1840–1928)

In an Underground Dressing-Station

Quietly they set their burden down: he tried
To grin; moaned; moved his head from side to side.

'O put my leg down, doctor, do!' (He'd got
A bullet in his ankle; and he'd been shot
Horribly through the guts.) The surgeon seemed
So kind and gentle, saying, above that crying,
'You *must* keep still, my lad.' But he was dying.

2 June 1917 (begun in April)

SIEGFRIED SASSOON (1886–1967)

In the Pink

So Davies wrote: 'This leaves me in the pink.'
Then scrawled his name: 'Your loving sweetheart, Willie.'
With crosses for a hug. He'd had a drink
Of rum and tea; and, though the barn was chilly,
For once his blood ran warm; he had pay to spend.
Winter was passing; soon the year would mend.

But he couldn't sleep that night; stiff in the dark
He groaned and thought of Sundays at the farm,
And how he'd go as cheerful as a lark
In his best suit, to wander arm in arm
With brown-eyed Gwen, and whisper in her ear
The simple, silly things she liked to hear.

And then he thought: to-morrow night we trudge
Up to the trenches, and my boots are rotten.
Five miles of stodgy clay and freezing sludge,
And everything but wretchedness forgotten.
To-night he's in the pink; but soon he'll die.
And still the war goes on – *he* don't know why.

10 February 1916

SIEGFRIED SASSOON (1886–1967)

Comparing poems

1 Look back at the poems by Robert Southey, Thomas Hardy and
   Siegfried Sassoon. Although the poets were all writing at different
   times about different wars they have similar feelings about war.

Copy the table below and complete it with evidence from each poet for
each statement:

	Southey	Hardy	Sassoon
War is a waste of life			
War causes unnecessary suffering			
War has nothing to do with ordinary people			

Response

1 In 'In the Pink' the soldier has just finished writing a letter. What do
   you think he wrote? Would he have told the truth about life in the
   trenches or would he have tried to cover up the facts so as not to
   upset his sweetheart? Write the soldier's letter using all the
   information in this poem and 'In an Underground Dressing-Station'
   to help you.

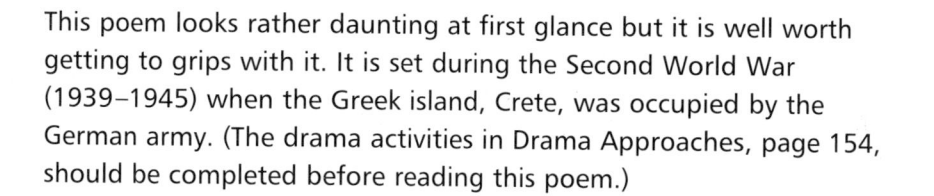

This poem looks rather daunting at first glance but it is well worth getting to grips with it. It is set during the Second World War (1939–1945) when the Greek island, Crete, was occupied by the German army. (The drama activities in Drama Approaches, page 154, should be completed before reading this poem.)

Death of an Aircraft

An incident of the Cretan campaign, 1941

1 One day on our village in the month of July
   An aeroplane sank from the sea of the sky,
      White as a whale it smashed on the shore
      Bleeding oil and petrol all over the floor.

2 The Germans advanced in the vertical heat
   To save the dead plane from the people of Crete,
      And round the glass wreck in a circus of snow
      Set seven mechanical sentries to go.

3 Seven stalking spiders about the sharp sun
   Clicking like clockwork and each with a gun,
      But at 'Come to the cookhouse' they wheeled about
      And sat down to sausages and sauerkraut.

4 Down from the mountain burning so brown
   Wriggled three heroes from Kastelo town,
      Deep in the sand they silently sank
      And each struck a match for a petrol tank.

5 Up went the plane in a feather of fire
   As the bubbling boys began to retire
      And, grey in the guardhouse, seven Berliners
      Lost their stripes as well as their dinners.

6 Down in the village, at murder-stations,
The Germans fell in friends and relations:
    But not a Kastelian snapped an eye
    As he spat in the air and prepared to die.

7 Not a Kastelian whispered a word
Dressed with the dust to be massacred,
    And squinted up at the sky with a frown
    As three bubbly boys came walking down.

8 One was sent to the county gaol
Too young for bullets if not for bail,
    But the other two were in prime condition
    To take on a load of ammunition.

9 In Archontiki they stood in the weather
Naked, hungry, chained together:
    Stark as the stones in the market place,
    Under the eyes of the populace.

10 Their irons unlocked as their naked hearts
They faced the squad and their funeral-carts.
    The Captain cried, 'Before you're away
    Is there any last word you'd like to say?'

11 'I want no words,' said one, 'with my lead,
Only some water to cool my head.'
    'Water,' the other said, 'is all very fine
    But I'll be taking a glass of wine.

12 A glass of wine for the afternoon
With permission to sing a signature tune'.
    And he ran the raki down his throat
    And took a deep breath for the leading note.

13 But before the squad could shoot or say
   Like the impala* he leapt away
      Over the rifles, under the biers,
      The bullets rattling round his ears.

14 'Run!' they cried to the boy of stone
   Who now stood there in the street alone,
      But, 'Rather than bring revenge on your head
      It is better for me to die,' he said.

15 The soldiers turned their machine-guns round
   And shot him down with a dreadful sound
      Scrubbed his face with perpetual dark
      And rubbed it out like a pencil mark.

16 But his comrade slept in the olive tree
   And sailed by night on the gnawing sea,
      The soldier's silver shilling earned
      And, armed like an archangel, returned.

* A kind of antelope

CHARLES CAUSLEY (1917–   )

● ● ● ● ● ● ● ● ● ● ● ●

Looking closely

1   This is a long poem and it helps to begin by sorting out what
    happened! Write one or two sentences to summarize what happened
    in each verse. Use these questions to help you:

    Verses 1–3   Where does the aeroplane crash?
                        Who does the aeroplane belong to?
                        What do the seven sentries have to do?
                        Why do they leave their position?

    Verses 4–7   What do the three boys do to the plane?
                        What happens to the sentries?

    Verses 8–12   What were the Germans trying to find out from
                        the boys' friends and relations?
                        What were the Germans doing to people who
                        wouldn't tell them anything?
                        Where were the boys sent?
                        What is about to happen to them?

    Verses 13–15   How does the boy escape?
                        Why does he wait to face his killers?

    Verse 16   What do you think has happened to the boy's
                        comrade?
                        What do you think the soldier's 'silver shilling' is?

2   Now look back at each group of verses and try to think of a title for
    each section. Be prepared to explain why you have chosen your titles.

3   Discuss these statements and rank them in order to say which you
    think is most true of the poem:
    ● The poem is about the cruelty of the Germans during the
      Second World War.
    ● The poem is about the courage of the Cretan people.
    ● The poem is about loyalty to friends and family.
    ● The poem is about bravery and heroism.
    ● The poem is about the fact that war is a waste of life.

Comparing poems

1   In groups read each of the poems again. Which poem do you
    think could be used most effectively in an anti-war campaign?
    Prepare reasons for your choice and share your decision with the
    rest of the class.

Response

1   War is always with us. What questions would you like to ask about
    a war that is going on in the world today?
    a   Make a list of your questions keeping each one as brief and to-
        the-point as possible.
    b   Now use your questions as the basis for a poem of your own
        about war.

7 The Rime of the Ancient Mariner

In this unit you will be looking at part of a long narrative poem, 'The Rime of the Ancient Mariner' by Samuel Taylor Coleridge (1772–1834). Coleridge was another of the Romantic Poets – you have already met Keats and Shelley in previous units. 'The Rime of the Ancient Mariner' was one of the three great poems Coleridge wrote, the other two being 'Christabel' and 'Kubla Khan'. Coleridge was addicted to the powerful drug, opium, which gave him fantastical dreams and visions, and so his poetry often has a dream-like feel to it. However, this poem was inspired by an actual dream told to Coleridge by a friend, the poet Wordsworth.

The Rime of the Ancient Mariner (extract)

The poem begins at a wedding. Suddenly, one of the guests is stopped by an old sailor who 'holds him with his glittering eye' and forces him to listen to his story. The old man tells the tale of how he set sail one fine day, heading south. All went well until:

> And now the Storm-blast came, and he
> Was tyrannous and strong:
> He struck with his o'ertaking wings,
> And chased us south along.
>
> With sloping masts and dipping prow,
> As who pursued with yell and blow
> Still treads the shadow of his foe
> And forward bends his head,
> The ship drove fast, loud roared the blast,
> And southward aye we fled.

And now there came both mist and snow,
And it grew wondrous cold:
And ice, mast-high, came floating by,
As green as emerald.

And through the drifts the snowy clifts
Did send a dismal sheen:
Now shapes of men nor beasts we ken –
The ice was all between.

The ice was here, the ice was there,
The ice was all around:
It cracked and growled, and roared and howled
Like noises in a swound!

At length did cross an Albatross:
Through the fog it came;
As if it had been a Christian soul,
We hailed it in God's name.

It ate the food it ne'er had eat,
And round and round it flew.
The ice did split with a thunder-fit;
The helmsman steered us through!

And a good south wind sprung up behind;
The Albatross did follow,
And every day, for food or play,
Came to the mariners' hollo!

● ● ● ● ● ● ● ● ● ● ●

In mist or cloud, on mast or shroud,
It perched for vespers nine;
Whiles all the night, through fog-smoke white,
Glimmered the white Moon-shine.

'God save thee, ancient Mariner!
From the fiends, that plague thee thus! –
Why look'st thou so?' – 'With my cross-bow
I shot the Albatross.

● ● ● ● ● ● ● ● ● ● ● ● ●

Drama

1 Why did the Ancient Mariner kill the Albatross?
Work as a whole class. One of you play the part of the Ancient
Mariner. The rest of the class should take on roles of sailors who
were present when the albatross was shot. One person needs to play
the part of the ship's captain – perhaps your teacher.

a Take turns to tell what has been happening on board ship since
you set sail. Then talk about what you witnessed when the
albatross was killed. Some of you may condemn the Ancient
Mariner when it is your turn to speak, some of you may feel that
he was right to kill the bird that brought the fog and mist. Decide
whether the Ancient Mariner should be allowed to speak in his
own defence.

b As a class decide what, if anything, you think should happen to
the Ancient Mariner.

2 Soundtrack

a Work in groups of five or six. You are going to create a
soundtrack to accompany three verses from the section you have
just read.

Choose which verses you would like to work with – they need *not* be
consecutive verses. Practise reading the verses aloud. Use as much
expression as possible to get across the meaning of your chosen verses.
Decide where you need to pause, and where you need to use a different
voice, or more than one voice.

b Now create a soundtrack to run underneath the reading. Through sound, describe the mood of the verses, and try to suggest a sense of place. As well as using your voices, think how you can use hands and feet effectively. Don't forget the importance of the occasional dramatic silence. If possible, borrow some musical instruments to use in your soundtrack.

c Put words and sounds together, making sure that your soundtrack does not overwhelm the words.

the poem continued ...

The ship sailed on out of the ice, northwards across the Pacific Ocean. And then the wind dropped, the ship was becalmed, and it grew hotter and hotter.

> Water, water, every where,
> And all the boards did shrink;
> Water, water, every where,
> Nor any drop to drink.

The sailors blamed the Ancient Mariner for their predicament – because he was the one who had shot their good-luck bird. They decided that the Ancient Mariner must be punished.

> Ah! well a-day! what evil looks
> Had I from old and young!
> Instead of the cross, the Albatross
> About my neck was hung.

The sailors continued to suffer under the blazing sun, unable to sail away because there was no wind.

There passed a weary time. Each throat
Was parched, and glazed each eye.
A weary time! a weary time!
How glazed each weary eye,
When looking westward I beheld,
A something in the sky.

At first it seemed a little speck,
And then it seemed a mist:
It moved and moved, and took at last
A certain shape, I wist.

A speck, a mist, a shape, I wist!
And still it neared and neared:
As if it dodged a water-sprite,
It plunged and tacked and veered.

With throats unslaked, with black lips baked,
We could not laugh nor wail;
Through utter drought all dumb we stood!
I bit my arm, I sucked the blood,
And cried, A sail! a sail!

With throats unslaked, with black lips baked,
Agape they heard me call:
Gramercy! they for joy did grin,
And all at once their breath drew in,
As they were drinking all.

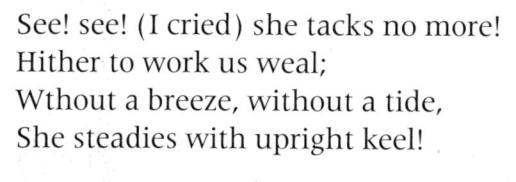

See! see! (I cried) she tacks no more!
Hither to work us weal;
Wthout a breeze, without a tide,
She steadies with upright keel!

The western wave was all a-flame,
The day was well-nigh done!
Almost upon the western wave
Rested the broad bright Sun;
When that strange shape drove suddenly
Betwixt us and the Sun.

In fact, the ship was a dreadful skeleton-ship, and on board were two ghastly figures, Death and Life-in-Death. Life-in-Death is described as follows:

Her lips were red, her looks were free,
Her locks were yellow as gold:
Her skin was as white as leprosy,
The night-Mare Life-in-Death was she,
Who thicks man's blood with cold.

Response

1 Write one verse of five lines to describe the other figure, Death. Try to use the same rhythm and rhyme pattern as Coleridge has used in his verse. You could begin:

   His lips were black, his eyes were …

Looking closely

1 Work in groups of four.

    a Divide between you this section of the poem so that each person in the group is responsible for one or two of the verses.

    b Work individually on your verses, making a note of any repetition of sounds or meaning. Note also how your verses make you feel, perhaps, for example, you feel hopeful or apprehensive?

    c Come together in your group to talk about your findings. Take turns to talk about the repeating patterns of sounds, words and phrases that you have discovered.

    d Plot a rough graph of the feelings you experience during this part, for example:

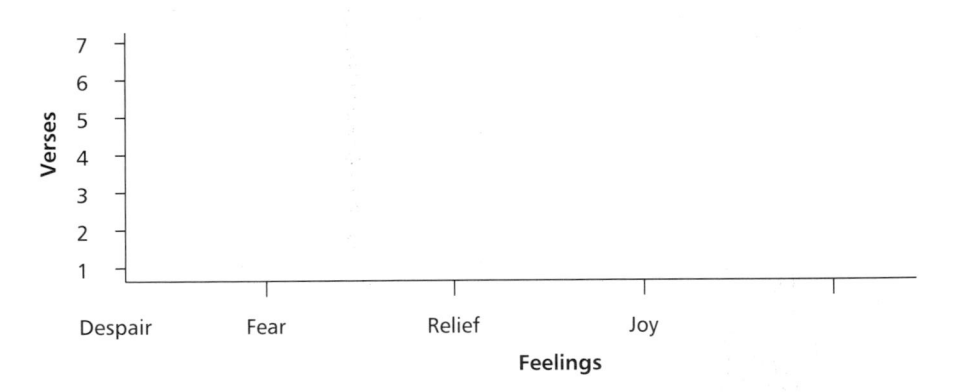

the poem continued ...

The skeleton ship pulled up alongside the other becalmed ship. The sun suddenly disappeared, and it was night. And then something really frightening happened.

> Four times fifty living men
> (And I heard nor sigh nor groan),
> With heavy thump, a lifeless lump,
> They dropped down one by one.
>
> The souls did from their bodies fly, –
> They fled to bliss or woe!
> And every soul, it passed me by,
> Like the whizz of my cross-bow!

And that is where we shall pause for a moment. The ship is unable to move; the sailors have all died; the Ancient Mariner is alone on the ship, still with the albatross round his neck. What do you think happens next?

Drama

1 Divide into pairs.

A is a television researcher gathering material for a programme which will be called, 'Strange Happenings at Sea'.

B is the Ancient Mariner who has somehow reached the safety of land.

B may, or may not, wish to reveal everything that happened after the death of his companions.

A should probe to find out how **B** survived, and how he reached land.

After the interviews, come together as a class.

Everyone who was **A** reports back their findings to the whole class.

the poem continued ...

For seven days and seven nights the Ancient Mariner remained on board ship, cursed by the cold stares in the eyes of the dead sailors.

> An orphan's curse would drag to hell
> A spirit from on high;
> But oh! more horrible than that
> Is the curse in a dead man's eye!
> Seven days, seven nights, I saw that curse,
> And yet I could not die.

But he was not the only creature left alive in that still ocean, for the water teemed with beautiful snakes.

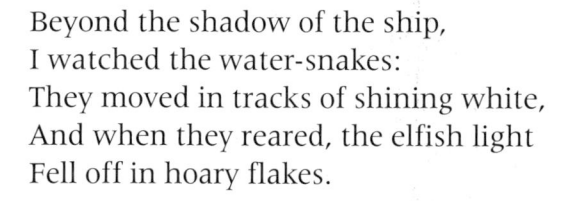

Beyond the shadow of the ship,
I watched the water-snakes:
They moved in tracks of shining white,
And when they reared, the elfish light
Fell off in hoary flakes.

Within the shadow of the ship
I watched their rich attire:
Blue, glossy green, and velvet black,
They coiled and swam; and every track
Was a flash of golden fire.

O happy living things! no tongue
Their beauty might declare:
A spring of love gushed from my heart,
And I blessed them unaware:
Sure my kind saint took pity on me,
And I blessed them unaware.

Suddenly, on the seventh day, the Ancient Mariner blessed these creatures that
God had made, and:

The self same moment I could pray;
And from my neck so free
The Albatross fell off, and sank
Like lead into the sea.

● ● ● ● ● ● ● ● ● ● ● ●

Once more the ship began to move through the water. But the ship was too large for the Ancient Mariner to manage on his own. Who do you think helped him?

The loud wind never reached the ship,
Yet now the ship moved on!
Beneath the lightning and the Moon
The dead men gave a groan.

They groaned, they stirred, they all uprose,
Nor spake, nor moved their eyes;
It had been strange, even in a dream,
To have seen those dead men rise.

The helmsman steered, the ship moved on;
Yet never a breeze up blew;
The mariners all 'gan work the ropes,
Where they were wont to do:

They raised their limbs like lifeless tools –
We were a ghastly crew.

The body of my brother's son
Stood by me, knee to knee:
The body and I pulled at one rope,
But he said nought to me.

Drama

1 Work in groups of five or six. Read the four verses on the previous page again very carefully. Talk about what happened on board ship. Now silently, working together slowly, show what happened as a short piece of mime. Move stiffly, and purposefully, almost as if you are mechanical figures, rather than real people. This should help you to create the dream-like feeling of this scene.

the poem continued ...

Finally the ship reached home, but just as it sailed within sight of the shore it suddenly sank beneath the waves taking the corpses of the dead sailors with it. The Ancient Mariner was saved from drowning, but as a punishment for what he had done, was forced to continually re-tell his story to whoever would listen.

8 Return to the Sea

(See **Drama Approaches**, page 155, for drama activities to be completed at the end of this unit.)

This unit opens with a very old poem, 'Sir Patrick Spens', which probably dates back 700 years to the thirteenth century. Not very much is known about the origins of these very old poems because many were passed on as songs and not written down until much later. It seems likely that the ballad of Sir Patrick Spens was based on a real shipwreck which took place either off the coast of Scotland or Norway.

Sir Patrick Spens

The king sits in Dunfermline town,
    Drinking the blood-red wine:
'O where will I get a skeely skipper,
    To sail this new ship of mine?'

O up and spake an eldern knight,
    Sat at the king's right knee:
'Sir Patrick Spens is the best sailor
    That ever sail'd the sea.'

Our king has written a braid letter,
    And seal'd it with his hand,
And sent it to Sir Patrick Spens,
    Was walking on the strand.

'To Noroway, to Noroway,
  To Noroway o'er the faem;
The king's daughter of Noroway,
  'Tis thou maun bring her hame.'

The first word that Sir Patrick read,
  Sae loud, loud laughèd he;
The neist word that Sir Patrick read,
  The tear blinded his e'e.

'O wha is this has done this deed,
  And tauld the king o' me,
To send me out at this time of the year
  To sail upon the sea?

Be it wind, be it weet, be it hail, be it sleet,
  Our ship must sail the faem;
The king's daughter of Noroway,
  'Tis we must fetch her hame.'

● ● ● ● ● ● ● ● ● ● ● ●

They hoysed their sails on Monenday morn,
   Wi' a' the speed they may;
They hae landed in Noroway,
   Upon a Wodensday.

They hadna been a week, a week
   In Noroway but twae,
When that the lords o'Noroway
   Began aloud to say:

'Ye Scottishmen spend a' our king's goud,
   And a' our queenis fee!'
'Ye lie, ye lie, ye liars loud,
   Fu' loud I hear ye lie!

For I brought as much white monie
   As gane my men and me,
And I brought a half fou o' gude red goud
   Out o'er the sea wi' me.

Make ready, make ready, my merry men a',
  Our gude ship sails the morn:'
'Now, ever alake! my master dear,
  I fear a deadly storm!

I saw the new moon late yestreen,
  Wi' the auld moon in her arm;
And if we gang to sea, master,
  I fear we'll come to harm.'

They hadna sailed a league, a league,
  A league but barely three,
When the lift grew dark, and the wind blew loud,
  And gurly grew the sea.

The ankers brak, and the topmasts lap,
  It was sic a deadly storm,
And the waves came o'er the broken ship,
  Till a' her sides were torn.

'O where will I get a gude sailor,
  To take my helm in hand,
Till I get up to the tall topmast,
  To see if I can spy land?'

'O here am I, a sailor gude,
  To take the helm in hand,
Till you go up to the tall topmast,
  But I fear you'll ne'er spy land.'

He hadna gane a step, a step,
  A step but barely ane,
When a bout flew out of our goodly ship,
  And the salt sea it cam in.

'Gae fetch a web o' the silken claith,
  Another o' the twine,
And wap them into our ship's side,
  And let na the sea come in.'

They fetched a web o' the silken claith,
  Another o' the twine,
And they wapped them roun' that gude ship's side,
  But still the sea cam in.

O laith, laith were our gude Scots lords
  To weet their cork-heel'd shoon;
But lang or a' the play was play'd,
  They wat their hats aboon.

And mony was the feather-bed
  That flottered on the faem,
And mony was the gude lord's son
  That never mair cam hame.

The ladies wrang their fingers white,
  The maidens tore their hair,
A' for the sake of their true loves,
  For them they'll see nae mair.

● ● ● ● ● ● ● ● ● ● ● ●

O lang, lang may the ladies sit,
  Wi' their fans into their hand,
Before they see Sir Patrick Spens
  Come sailing to the strand.

And lang, lang may the maidens sit,
  Wi' their goud kames in their hair,
A' waiting for their ain dear loves,
  For them they'll see nae mair.

Half owre, half owre to Aberdour
  'Tis fifty fathoms deep,
And there lies gude Sir Patrick Spens,
  Wi' the Scots lords at his feet.

● ● ● ● ● ● ● ● ● ● ● ●

Looking closely

1   At first glance this poem seem difficult because it is written as it
    would have been spoken – in Scottish dialect.

    Read the poem aloud. It will be easier to understand the meaning of
    the unfamiliar words when you say them: for example, Wodnesday is
    very like its meaning, Wednesday.

2   'Sir Patrick Spens' is a **ballad**. A ballad is a poem that tells a story in
    a particular form. Originally ballads were often sung, and many still
    appear as songs today.
    Look at the ballad form:
    ● Each verse has the same number of lines. Do the same lines
      rhyme in each verse?
    ● The ballad has a very definite rhythm. Choose one verse to read
      aloud, and as you read exaggerate the beat of the lines – almost
      as if you were half-singing, half-speaking the lines.

Response

1   In groups produce a reading performance of the first four verses of
    the poem. Divide the poem into the following parts:

    Narrator   King   Knight   Sir Patrick Spens (reading letter)

    Think about the personalities of the king and the knight before you
    decide how their lines should be read.

● ● ● ● ● ● ● ● ● ● ● ●

The Yarn of the *Nancy Bell*

'Twas on the shores that round our coast
   From Deal to Ramsgate span,
That I found alone on a piece of stone
   An elderly naval man.

His hair was weedy, his beard was long,
   And weedy and long was he,
And I heard this wight on the shore recite,
   In a singular minor key:

'Oh, I am a cook and a captain bold,
   And the mate of the *Nancy* brig,
And a bo'sun tight, and a midshipmite,
   And the crew of the captain's gig.'

And he shook his fists and he tore his hair,
   Till I really felt afraid,
For I couldn't help thinking the man had been drinking,
   And so I simply said:

'Oh, elderly man, it's little I know
   Of the duties of men of the sea,
And I'll eat my hand if I understand
   However you can be

●　●　●　●　●　●　●　●　●　●　●　●

'At once a cook, and a captain bold,
　And the mate of the *Nancy* brig,
And a bo'sun tight, and a midshipmite,
　And the crew of the captain's gig.'

Then he gave a hitch to his trousers, which
　Is a trick all seamen larn,
And having got rid of a thumping quid,
　He spun this painful yarn:

''Twas in the good ship *Nancy Bell*
　That we sailed to the Indian Sea,
And there on a reef we come to grief,
　Which has often occurred to me.

'And pretty nigh all the crew was drowned
　(There was seventy-seven o' soul),
And only ten of the *Nancy's* men
　Said "Here!" to the muster-roll.

'There was me and the cook and the captain bold,
　And the mate of the *Nancy* brig,
And the bo'sun tight, and a midshipmite,
　And the crew of the captain's gig.

'For a month we'd neither wittles not drink,
　Till a-hungry we did feel,
So we drawed a lot, and, accordin' shot
　The captain for our meal.

'The next lot fell to the *Nancy's* mate,
  And a delicate dish he made;
Then our appetite with the midshipmite
  We seven survivors stayed.

'And then we murdered the bo'sun tight,
  And he much resembled pig;
Then we wittled free, did the cook and me,
  On the crew of the captain's gig.

'Then only the cook and me was left,
  And the delicate question, "Which
Of us two goes to the kettle?" arose,
  And we argued it out as sich.

'For I loved that cook as a brother, I did,
  And the cook he worshipped me;
But we'd both be blowed if we'd either be stowed
  In the other chap's hold, you see.

' "I'll be eat if you dines off me," says Tom;
  "Yes, that," says I, "you'll be, –
" I'm boiled if I die, my friend," quoth I;
  And "Exactly so," quoth he.

● ● ● ● ● ● ● ● ● ● ● ●

'Says he, "Dear James, to murder me
   Were a foolish thing to do,
For don't you see that you can't cook *me*,
   While I can – and will – cook *you*!"

'So he boils the water, and takes the salt
   And the pepper in portions true
(Which he never forgot), and some chopped shalot,
   And some sage and parsley too.

"Come here," says he, with a proper pride,
   Which his smiling features tell,
' "Twill soothing be if I let you see
   How extremely nice you'll smell."

'And he stirred it round and round and round,
   And he sniffed at the foaming froth;
When I ups with his heels, and smothers his squeals
   In the scum of the boiling broth.

'And I eat that cook in a week or less,
   And – as I eating be
The last of his chops, why, I almost drops,
   For a wessel in sight I see!

● ● ● ● ● ● ● ● ● ● ● ●

'And I never larf, and I never smile,
    And I never lark nor play,
But sit and croak, and a single joke
    I have – which is to say:

'"Oh, I am a cook and a captain bold,
    And the mate of the *Nancy* brig,
And a bo'sun tight, and amidshipmite,
    And the crew of the captain's gig!" '

W S GILBERT (1836–1911)

Looking closely

1 Our first poem in this unit, 'Sir Patrick Spens', is an old ballad. In the nineteenth century many poets imitated the ballad form in their work.

Working with a partner, decide whether you think this poem is also a ballad. Here are some points to help you reach your decision:

a Does the poem tell a story?

b Does the poem tell a *tragic* story?

c Do all the verses contain the same number of lines?

d Is there a strong, regular rhythm to each verse?

e What is the rhyme pattern of the poem?

2 Write your own ballad poem.

a First, plan your story. You don't need to set it in the past – it could be about something that could happen to you, like going to a football match or going on holiday.

b Decide how many verses you are going to have. Plan what will happen in each verse.

c Write your ballad. Write in ballad form with the same number of lines in each verse and a regular rhythm and rhyme pattern.

Some ballads have **refrains** which repeat the same lines at the end of every verse. You might like to include a 'refrain' in your ballad.

● ● ● ● ● ● ● ● ● ● ● ●

The Shell

And then I pressed the shell
Close to my ear.
And listened well.
And straightway, like a bell,
Came low and clear
The slow, sad murmur of far distant seas
Whipped by an icy breeze
Upon a shore
Wind-swept and desolate.
It was a sunless strand that never bore
The footprint of a man,
Nor felt the weight
Since time began
Of any human quality or stir,
Save what the dreary winds and waves incur.

And in the hush of waters was the sound
Of pebbles, rolling round,
For ever rolling, with a hollow sound;
And bubbling sea-weeds, as the waters go,
Swish to and fro
Their long, cold tentacles of slimy grey;
There was no day;
Nor ever came a night
Setting the stars alight
To wonder at the moon:

● ● ● ● ● ● ● ● ● ● ● ● ●

Was twilight only, and the frightened croon,
Smitten to whimpers, of the dreary wind
And waves that journeyed blind…
And then I loosed my ear, Oh, it was sweet
To hear a cart go jolting down the street.

JAMES STEPHENS (1859–1892)

Looking closely

1 a 'The Shell' is a poem of carefully chosen sounds and rhythm.
      Read the poem aloud.
      ● How do the lengths of the lines help to create the pattern of
        the waves?
      ● Can you hear the hissing of the waves as they run up the
        shore, and then retreat back, rasping across the pebbles?
   b Make a list of all the words in the poem which contain definite
      sounds, for example 'hu*sh* of waters'.

Words with a sound that matches their meaning are called
onomatopoeic words.

Response

1 Write your own onomatopoeic poem about a thunderstorm.

   Begin by making a list of as many useful sound words as possible,
   for example, roar, crash, spit. Use a **thesaurus** to help you find
   new words.

Song of the Sea and People

Shell of the conch* was sounded,
sounded like foghorn.
Women rushed to doorways,
to fences, to gateways, and watched.
Canoe made from cotton tree
came sailing shoulder high, from up
mountain-pass down to the sea.
   They stared
      at many men under canoe.
   The mothers and children stared.

Shell of the conch was sounded,
sounded like foghorn.
Women rushed to seaside.
Canoes had come in,
come in from way out
of big sea, loaded
with fish, crabs and lobsters.
   They stared
      at sea-catch.
   The mothers and children stared.

Shell of the conch was sounded,
sounded like foghorn.
Women rushed to seaside.

● ● ● ● ● ● ● ● ● ● ● ●

Canoe out of cotton tree had thrown men,
thrown them into deep sea.
Deep sea swallowed men.
Big sea got boat back.
     They stared
     at empty canoe.
     The mothers and children stared.

J<small>AMES</small> B<small>ERRY</small> (1924–   )

*Conch is the spiral shell of a kind of shellfish, sometimes used as a horn.

(see Drama Approaches, page 155)

Looking closely

1 What are your first impressions of this poem? Where do you think
   it is set?
2 In 'Song of the Sea and People' the pattern of each verse is the same.
   Some of the lines are the same while some are changed slightly.
   What effect does this have?

Response

1 a Write two lines to describe a storm at sea. Choose your words
      very carefully; perhaps include some onomatopoeic words.
   b In groups arrange all your lines into a sequence. Try different
      sequences of lines. You might record your work and then replay it
      to decide which order of lines sounds most effective.
   c When you have decided on your final sequence write out your
      poem for display.

9 Choices

We all make choices every day; the ability to choose is something all human beings share. But choice and choosing are complicated matters – some people have always had more choice than others.

The poem 'Ain't I a Woman?' was written in 1852. It describes how at the time, black women had no rights, no choices.

A few years later, in 1866, a white woman, who had never known any of the hardships described by Sojourner Truth, was also writing about choice; about the princess who died waiting to be chosen. The poet was a famous Victorian, Christina Rossetti.

The rest of the poems in this unit are all modern, and are all written by women.

Ain't I a Woman?

That man over there say
a woman needs to be helped into carriages
and lifted over ditches
and to have the best place everywhere.
Nobody ever helped me into carriages
or over mud puddles
or gives me a best place…

and ain't I a woman?
Look at me
Look at my arm!
I have plowed and planted
and gathered into barns
and no man could head me…
And ain't I a woman?
I could work as much
and eat as much as a man –
when I could get to it –

Sojourner Truth

●　●　●　●　●　●　●　●　●　●　●　●

and bear the lash as well
and ain't I a woman?
I have born thirteen children
and seen most all sold into slavery
and when I cried out a mother's grief
none but Jesus heard me…
and ain't I a woman?
that little man in black there say
a woman can't have as much rights as a man
cause Christ wasn't a woman
Where did your Christ come from?
From God and a woman!
Man had nothing to do with him!
If the first woman God ever made
was strong enough to turn the world
upside down all alone
together women ought to be able to turn it
rightside up again.

SOJOURNER TRUTH (1797–1883)

Response

1 This speech by Sojourner Truth was made at a Women's Rights
convention in America.

Read the poem aloud as if you are Sojourner Truth making that
speech. After reading, say how the poem made you feel – powerful?
bitter? helpless? angry? or a different emotion?

Is it possible to read the poem differently, as a lullaby perhaps? Or
does the content of the poem make it impossible to read in any way
other than as a speech?

The Prince's Progress (extract)

Too Late

Too late for love, too late for joy,
  Too late, too late!
You loiter'd on the road too long,
  You trifled at the gate:
The enchanted dove upon her branch
  Died without a mate;
The enchanted princess in her tower
  Slept, died, behind the grate;
Her heart was starving all this while
  You made it wait.

CHRISTINA ROSSETTI (1830–1894)

Response

1 **a** Think about what may have happened before this extract begins.
      Talk with a partner about:
      ● Why the prince had delayed, or been delayed.
      ● Why the princess was waiting for the prince.
   b Write a short fairy story based on the poem. Your story must try
      to answer the questions you have discussed.
   c Now write the same story, but as a modern romance. Who will
      your prince and princess become; perhaps the lead singer from
      a famous band and a rich, young woman who lives at home with
      her film star parents (the king and queen)? Your story must still
      answer questions **a** and **b**. Can you write the same ending?
      When you have finished writing, ask yourself if the story is at all
      believable.

● ● ● ● ● ● ● ● ● ● ● ● ●

The Choosing

We were first equal Mary and I
with same coloured ribbons in mouse-coloured
  hair

and with equal shyness,
we curtseyed to the lady councillor
for copies of Collins' Children's Classics.
First equal, equally proud.

Best friends too Mary and I
a common bond in being cleverest
  (equal)
in our small school's small class.
I remember
the competition for top desk
at school service.
And my terrible fear
of her superiority at sums.

I remember the housing scheme
where we both stayed.
The same houses, different homes,
where the choices were made.

I don't know exactly why they moved,
but anyway they went.
Something about a three-apartment
and a cheaper rent.

But from the top deck of the high-school bus
I'd glimpse among the others on the corner
Mary's father, mufflered, contrasting strangely
with the elegant greyhounds by his side.

He didn't believe in high school education,
especially for girls,
or in forking out for uniforms.

Ten years later on a Saturday –
I am coming from the library –
sitting near me on the bus,
Mary
with a husband who is tall,
curly haired, has eyes
for no one else but Mary.
Her arms are round the full-shaped vase
that is her body.
Oh, you can see where the attraction lies
in Mary's life –
not that I envy her, really.

And I am coming from the library
with my arms full of books.
I think of those prizes that were ours for
    the taking
and wonder when the choices got made
we don't remember making.

LIZ LOCHHEAD (1947–   )

Response

1   At the end of the poem, Liz Lochhead says that she wonders 'when
    the choices got made'.

    Work in small groups. Each of you take turns to be Mary. Try to
    describe to the others a moment in your life when you felt an
    important choice was made. Who made the choice? The rest of the
    group can help Mary by asking questions where necessary.

Overheard in County Sligo

I married a man from County Roscommon
and I live at the back of beyond
with a field of cows and a yard of hens
and six white geese on the pond.

At my door's a square of yellow corn
caught up by its corners and shaken,
and the road runs down through the open gate
and freedom's there for the taking.

I had thought to work on the Abbey stage
or have my name in a book,
to see my thought on the printed page,
or still the crowd with a look.

But I turn to fold the breakfast cloth
and to polish the lustre and brass,
to order and dust the tumbled rooms
and find my face in the glass.

I ought to feel I'm a happy woman
for I lie in the lap of the land,
and I married a man from County Roscommon
and I live in the back of beyond.

GILLIAN CLARKE (1937–)

Woman Work

I've got the children to tend
The clothes to mend
The floor to mop
The food to shop
Then the chicken to fry
The baby to dry
I got company to feed
The garden to weed
I've got the shirts to press
The tots to dress
The cane to be cut
I gotta clean up this hut
Then see about the sick
And the cotton to pick.

Shine on me, sunshine
Rain on me, rain
Fall softly, dewdrops
And cool my brow again.

Storm, blow me from here
With your fiercest wind
Let me float across the sky
'Til I can rest again.

Fall gently, snowflakes
Cover me with white
Cold icy kisses and
Let me rest tonight.

Sun, rain, curving sky
Mountain, oceans, leaf and stone
Star shine, moon glow
You're all that I can call my own.

MAYA ANGELOU (1928–   )

Looking closely

1   These two poems seem to be about women who are trapped by
   their circumstances. What exactly do the women have in common?
   What are the differences between them? Copy out and complete the
   table below as fully as possible.

Overheard in County Sligo	Woman Work
Similarities	
The woman lives in a rural area	The woman lives in a country area where cane and cotton crops are grown
Differences	
The woman does not mention children.	

Ever So Cute

Little boy dressed in his white judo suit,
Little black belt looking ever so cute.
Hush! Hush! Whisper who dares!
Christopher Robin can throw you downstairs.

Go on Mummy, it's only ten –
I want to watch *Dracula's Bride* again.
It's ever so good when he bites ladies' necks –
Me and my teddy like violence and sex.

And when it's over I want to play
The video game we bought today.
Shooting down spaceships. Bleep, bleep, bleep! Kill, kill!
I'll score three million and Dad will get nil.

Little boy growing so sturdy and tough –
Better not argue or he'll cut up rough.
Hush! Hush! Whatever you say,
Christopher Robin will get his own way.

WENDY COPE (1945–   )

● ● ● ● ● ● ● ● ● ● ● ●

Response

1   A **parody** is a poem which copies another poem, in order to make fun of the original.

   a   Find a copy of the original Christopher Robin poem, which Wendy Cope's poem parodies. It is a famous poem, and you may know it already.

   Work with a partner. Take it in turns to read aloud a verse from the original poem, and a verse from 'Ever So Cute'. Which words remain the same in both poems?

   b   Write the same sort of poem about a little girl, in which the little girl is the complete opposite of the boy. He is, or chooses to be, or is expected to be violent and tough; she must be weak and passive. You could begin:

   Little girl clothed in her pink frilly dress,
   Little curls shining, hair never a mess.

Comparing poems

1   a   Look back at all six poems in this unit.
   Complete the following statement for each poem.
   I like this poem because ...

   b   Mix up the order of your statements and read them aloud to a partner. Take turns to guess which poem is being described each time. When you are writing your statements, don't make them too obvious or easy to guess!

10 Sometimes School

William Blake, the second poet writing in this unit, was born in 1757 and died in 1827. He was one of a group of poets known as the Romantic Poets. Like all Romantic Poets, Blake believed that the imagination was terribly important, much more important than the logical reasoning which formal education encouraged. As you can see, some of his feelings about school are echoed by modern poets writing two centuries later.

Winter

On Winter mornings in the playground
The boys stand huddled,
Their cold hands doubled
Into trouser pockets.
The air hangs frozen
About the buildings
And the cold is an ache in the blood
And a pain on the tender skin
Beneath finger nails.
The odd shouts
Sound off like struck iron
And the sun
Balances white
Above the boundary wall.
I fumble my bus ticket
Between numb fingers
Into a fag,
Take a drag
And blow white smoke
Into the December air.

GARETH OWEN (1936–)

● ● ● ● ● ● ● ● ● ● ● ●

Looking closely

1 a Pick out all the words in this poem that are to do with cold and winter.
  b How does the poem make you feel about winter mornings? How does it make you feel about school?

The Schoolboy

I love to rise in a summer morn,
When the birds sing on every tree;
The distant huntsman winds his horn,
And the sky-lark sings with me.
O! what sweet company.

But to go to school in a summer morn,
O! it drives all joy away;
Under a cruel eye outworn,
The little ones spend the day
In sighing and dismay.

Ah! then at times I drooping sit,
And spend many an anxious hour,
Nor in my book can I take delight,
Nor sit in learning's bower,
Worn thro' with the dreary shower.

How can the bird that is born for joy,
Sit in a cage and sing?
How can a child, when fears annoy,
But droop his tender wing,
And forget his youthful spring?

O! father and mother, if buds are nipp'd,
And blossoms blown away,
And if the tender plants are stripp'd
Of their joy in the springing day,
By sorrow and care's dismay,

How shall the summer arise in joy
Or the summer fruits appear?
Or how shall we gather what griefs destroy
Or bless the mellowing year,
When the blasts of winter appear?

WILLIAM BLAKE (1757–1827)

● ● ● ● ● ● ● ● ● ● ●

Looking closely

1 After reading the poem what are your reactions to the schoolboy?
  Do you feel sorry for him?

  Blake has used **imagery** to help create a picture of the way the boy
  is feeling. Let's look at how the imagery works.

  Looking again at the first four verses in the poem produce two
  drawings. In each drawing, draw the boy on one side of your page
  and the bird opposite.

  ● Draw the bird and the boy from verse one.
  ● Draw the bird and the boy from verses three and four.

  What are the connections between the bird and the boy? What do
  you think Blake is saying about school?

Response

1 a In small groups discuss how *you* feel about school. You might
    find it difficult to reach an agreement about your likes and
    dislikes, but try to come to general conclusions that represent the
    views of the group.

  Use a table like this to organize your answers:

Good things about school	Bad things about school

  b Working alone, write two letters to William Blake. In the first,
    write about why you agree with the point of view he expresses in
    the poem. In the second, write about why you disagree.

Writing

and then i saw it
saw it all   all the mess
and blood and evrythink
and mam agenst the kichin dor
the flor all stiky
and the wall all wet
and red an dad besid the kichen draw
i saw it saw it all
an wrot it down an ever word of it is tru

You must take care to write in sentences,
Check your spellings and your paragraphs.
Is this finished? It is rather short.
Perhaps next time you will have more to say.

JAN DEAN

Comparing poems

1   In 'Writing' what point do you think the poet is trying to make
    about the imaginary teacher? Can you see any similarities between
    Jan Dean's and William Blake's views about education?

The Lesson

'Your father's gone,' my bald headmaster said.
His shiny dome and brown tobacco jar
Splintered at once in tears. It wasn't grief.
I cried for knowledge which was bitterer
Than any grief. For there and then I knew
That grief has uses – that a father dead
Could bind the bully's fist a week or two;
And then I cried for shame, then for relief.

I was a month past ten when I learnt this:
I still remember how the noise was stilled
In school-assembly when my grief came in.
Some goldfish in a bowl quietly sculled
Around their shining prison on its shelf.
They were indifferent. All the other eyes
Were turned towards me. Somewhere in myself
Pride, like a goldfish, flashed a sudden fin.

EDWARD LUCIE-SMITH (1933–   )

Looking closely

1 This poem is written from the boy's point of view. When the boy
found out about his father's death, he felt lots of different emotions.
Why do you think the boy had so many different feelings? Use the
chart below to help you focus your discussion.

The boy felt shame when.....................because.............................

The boy felt relief when.........................because..

The boy felt grief for............................during..

The boy felt pride because...

Response

1 Put yourself in the place of the headmaster in the poem and try to
imagine what he may have felt. Look at the words the headmaster
chose to tell the boy that his father had died.

Write the headmaster's diary: one entry for the day he broke the
news, and a second entry for the day the boy cried in assembly.

In each entry write a brief account of what actually happened,
followed by a longer account of how the headmaster felt.
Write in the first person – *you* are the headmaster.

● ● ● ● ● ● ● ● ● ● ● ● ●

He who owns the Whistle, rules the World

january wind and the sun
playing truant again.
Rain beginning to scratch
its fingernails across
the blackboard sky

in the playground
kids divebomb, corner
at silverstone or execute
traitors. Armed
with my Acme Thunderer
I step outside,
take a deep breath
and bring the world
to a standstill

ROGER McGOUGH (1937–   )

Response

1 **a** Think back to the time you spent in your primary school. Think
about a particular incident or event that you remember very
clearly. It could be something funny or frightening or puzzling.
   b Write about the incident. Write quickly for about ten minutes.
   c Look back at what you have written and underline the most vivid
and important points.
   d Rewrite your story as a poem. Try to include images of thoughts
and feelings which make the incident special to you.

11 Heroes for All Time

This unit is about two legendary heroes; heroes whose stories have been handed down through the centuries to the present day.

Beowulf is the first hero, and his story has been around possibly since the sixth century, and it is certainly well over one thousand years old!

The second hero is Sir Gawain, one of King Arthur's knights. The stories of King Arthur and his knights had also been popular for many centuries before the poem Sir Gawain and the Green Knight was finally written down towards the end of the fourteenth century – six hundred years ago. The fourteenth century version of Sir Gawain has been included, as well as a modern translation.

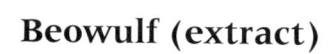

Beowulf (extract)

*Long ago, in Denmark, lived a powerful king, Hrothgar, who built a magnificent
hall which he named Heorot. The hall was a place where men could gather
together to feast and make merry. But also living in Denmark was the monster:*

> Grendel, the fiend's name: grim, infamous
> Wasteland stalker, master of the moor and the fen fortress.

*One night, as all Hrothgar's men lay sleeping in the hall, Grendel burst through
the doors and:*

> Grasped thirty warriors, and away he was homeward,
> Glutlusty with booty, laden with the slain.

*When the hero, Beowulf, heard what had happened, he was determined to
destroy this monster. So he and a handful of men lay in wait in the hall of
Heorot. As darkness fell, one by one the men slept, until only Beowulf remained
on guard. And then:*

Part 1

> Gliding through the shadows came the
> walker in the night.
> The warriors slept – all except one,
> And this man kept an unblinking watch.
> He waited, pent-heart swelling with anger 'gainst his foe
> From off the moorlands' misting fells
> Came Grendel stalking.

He moved through the dark, saw the perfect clearness
The gold panelled hall, mead-drinking place of men.
The door gave way at a touch of his hands.
Rage-inflamed, wreckage-bent, he tore the hall's jaws.
Hastening onwards, angrily advancing,
From his eyes shot a light in unlovely form of fire.
He saw in the hall the host of young warriors
And in his heart exulted, horrible monster,
All his hopes swelling to a gluttonous meal.
He meant to divide, monstrous in frightfulness,
The life from each body that lay in that place.

Part 2

As a first step he set his greedy hands on
A sleeping soldier, savagely tore him,
Gnashed to his bone-joints, bolted huge gobbets,
Sucked at his veins, and had soon eaten
All of the man, to his fingers and feet.
Then he moved forward, reached to seize our warrior Beowulf,
Stretched out for him with his spite filled fist:
But the faster man forestalling, rose up upon his arm
And quickly gripped that sickening hand.
The upholder of evils immediately knew
He had not met on middle earth's acres
With any other man of a harder hand-grasp.
He strained to be off, he ailed for his darkness,
His company of devils and his den beneath the mere;
But Hygelac's brave Kinsman recalled his
evening's utterance
And tightened his hold till fingers burst.

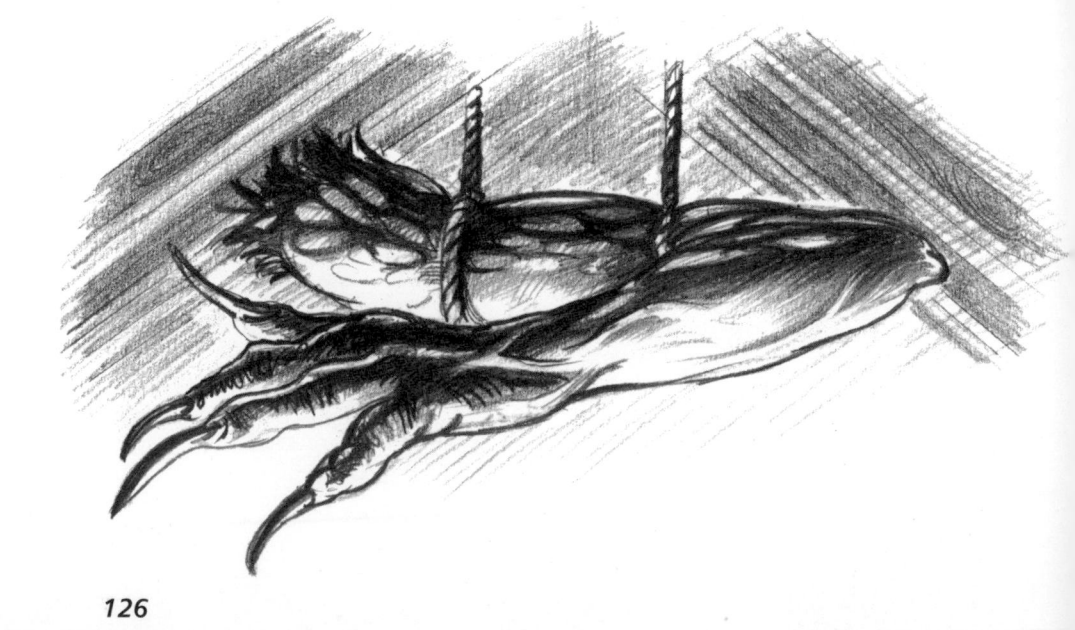

Part 3

It was then that this monster, moved by spite
   'gainst our race,
Found in the end flesh and bone were to fail him;
For Hygelac's great kinsman, stout-hearted warrior,
Had him fast by the hand; and hateful to each
Was the breath of the other.
A rip in the giant flesh-frame showed then,
Shoulder-muscles sprang apart, a snapping of
Tendons, bone-locks burst;
The arm of the demon was severed from his side,
And Grendel flew, death sick, to his joyless den
Where he knew that the end of his life was in sight.
Beowulf had cleansed Heorot, saved the hall
from persecution.

Part 4

As a signal to all the hero hung the hand,
The arm and torn-off shoulder, the entire limb,
Grendel's whole grip, beneath the soaring roof.

● ● ● ● ● ● ● ● ● ● ● ●

Response

1 a Summarize what happened:
- in Part 1 in one sentence
- in Part 2 in two sentences
- in Part 3 in two sentences
- in Part 4 in once sentence.

b Use your summaries of the action of the poem to produce a comic strip to tell the story of Beowulf and Grendel.

You will need about six frames. Leave a space underneath each frame for a caption. Use words from the poem to caption your comic strip.

Although there is no dialogue in the poem, you could invent some of your own and add speech bubbles to the pictures.

2 Beowulf was originally written in **Old English**, English that was in use about one thousand years ago. Another name for Old English is Anglo-Saxon.

Old English, which is also known as Anglo-Saxon, was very different from modern English.

Often **compound words** were used where we would use one word. A compound word is a word made up of more than one part.

These Old English compounds were very descriptive, for example: 'Swan-rad', meant *swan-riding – where the swan rides*, in modern English, *the sea*.

a Try to guess what these words meant. Say the words aloud to help you:
ban-hus, woruld-candel, beado-leoma
(The answers are printed upside down below.)

ban-hus = bone-house or body, woruld-candel = world candle or sun,
beado-leoma = battle-light or sword

● ● ● ● ● ● ● ● ● ● ● ●

b Look at the following short extract from 'Beowulf'. It is the original Old English for two of the lines to be found in Part 1. Try to match the original English with the modern translation.

Đā cōm of mōre under misthleoþum
Grendel gongan.

3 After Beowulf had defeated Grendel his troubles were not over. If Grendel had seemed a formidable enemy, his mother coming to seek revenge for the death of her son, was a nightmare come true.

Write the story of the struggle between Beowulf and Grendel's mother. Here are two lines from the poem to start you thinking:

'In the chilling currents, dwelling in dread waters,
The monstress ogress – Grendel's Mother'

● ● ● ● ● ● ● ● ● ● ● ● ●

4 The phrases below have all been taken from a later section of the poem. In this part of the poem, Beowulf has to fight against a terrible dragon.

Working with a partner, arrange a selection of the phrases to form a poem.

You may want to add some lines and phrases of your own so that the poem makes sense.

his neck between bitter fangs

spat death-fire

guard for all time

the hero's sword shattered

the grey ground boomed

three hundred winters

brought down such a stroke

or die in the fight

belched glowing fla[me]

hacked the dragon in half

precautions of chain-mail and shield

the war-seasoned King

(The first four drama activities in **Drama Approaches**, pages 156–157, should be completed *before* reading the poem.)

Sir Gawain and the Green Knight (extract)

þ pronounced 'th'; ʒ pronounced 'h'; u sometimes pronounced 'v'

The grene knyʒt vpon grounde grayþely hym dresses,
arranges,

A littel lut with þe hede, þe lere he discouerez,
    bent   *flesh*   *reveal*

His longe louelych lokkez he layd ouer his croun,
         lovely

Let be naked nec to þe note schewe.
              in readiness

Gauan gripped to his ax, and gederes hit on hyʒt,
                 raises

þe kay fot on þe folde he before sette,
   left   *ground*

Let hit down lyʒtly lyʒt on þe naked,
            lie

þat þe scharp of þe schalk schyndered þe bones,
   sharp-weapon   *man*   *shattered*

And schrank þurʒ þe schyire grece, and scade hit in twynne,
   sank deep through   *white*   *flesh*   *severed*

þat þe bit of þe broun stel bot on þe grounde
    edge   *bright* *steel* *bit*

þe fayre hede fro þe halce hit to þe erþe,
         neck

þat fele hit foyned wyth her fete, þere hit forth roled;
men   spurned   their   where

þe blod brayed fro þe body. þat blykked on þe grene;
burst   gleamed

And nawþer faltered ne fel þe freke neuer þe helder,
neither   knight never   the more

Bot styþly he start forth vpon styf schonkes,
strongly   steady legs

And runyschly he raȝt out, þere as renkkez stoden,
knights   stood

Laȝt to his lufly hed, and lyft hit vp sone;
seized   immediately

And syþen boȝez to his blonk, þe brydel he cachchez,
then   turns   horse

Steppez into stelbawe and strydez alofte,
stirrup   strode

And his hede by þe here in his honde haldez

And as sadly þe segge hym in his sadel sette
steadily   man   sat

As non unhap had hym ayled, þaȝ hedlez he were in stedde.
though headless   there

> He brayde his bulk aboute,
> *turned   body*
>
> þat vgly bodi þat bledde,
> *gruesome*
>
> Moni on of hym had doute,
> *Many   fear*
>
> Bi þat his resounȝ were redde.
> *By the time that words   declared*

On the ground the Green Knight graciously stood,
With head slightly slanting to expose the flesh.
His long and lovely locks he laid over his crown,
Neatly showing the naked neck, nape and all.
Gawain gripped his axe and gathered it on high,
Advanced the left foot before him on the ground,
And slashed swiftly down on the exposed part,
So that the sharp blade sheared through, shattering the bone,
Sank deep in the sleek flesh, split it in two,
And the scintillating steel struck the ground.
The fair head fell from the neck. On the floor it rolled,
So that people spurned and parried it as it passed their feet.
The blood spurted from the body, bright against the green.
Yet the fellow did not fall, nor falter one whit,
But stoutly strode forward on legs still sturdy
To where the worthy knights stood, weirdly reached out,
Seized his splendid head and straightway lifted it.
Then he strode to his steed, snatched the bridle,
Stepped into the stirrup and swung aloft,
Holding his head by the hair in his hand.
He settled himself in the saddle as steadily
As if nothing had happened to him, though he had
                         No head.
                 He twisted his trunk about,
                 That gruesome body that bled;
                 He caused much dread and doubt
                 By the time his say was said.

TRANSLATED BY BRIAN STONE

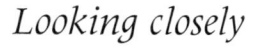

Looking closely

1   Look at the original version of 'Sir Gawain and the Green Knight',
    written in **Middle English**.

It is more like the language we use today than Old English. Notice how
many Middle English words are the same as their modern English
equivalent, simply spelled differently. For example, 'grene' is now
spelled 'green'.

Write down the other changes in spelling you can find:

Middle English	Modern English

Response

1 a This extract from the poem is full of repeated sounds, or
alliteration, for example:

long and lovely locks

Try reading sections of the poem aloud and really emphasizing the
alliteration. There are parts where you can almost hear that axe
cutting through flesh and bone, or the sound of steel on a stone
floor!

   b Prepare a reading of the poem in groups. Choose eight lines that
you all enjoy.

   One of you should be the narrator, while the rest of the group join
   in with the alliterative sounds so they really ring out.

2 Write a paragraph describing a fight between two knights. Try to
recreate the actual sounds of the fight by using as much alliteration
as possible, for example:

The steel sword shone sharply in the sunlight

3 Work in groups to explore one of the heroes in this unit.
   a Decide which figure you wish to work on.
   b On a very large sheet of paper draw round one member of your
group and cut out the outline.
   c Add features and other details to represent your chosen
character.
   d Look back over the poem. Inside your figure write down
everything you know about this character.
   e Pin your drawings to the wall and discuss ways in which they are
similar and dissimilar.

12 Two Scenes in Time

The two poems in this unit were written by Romantic Poets. The Romantics were a group of poets who were concerned with the world of feelings and the imagination. Both poets lived at about the same time; Shelley was born in 1792 and died in 1822, John Clare was born in 1793 and died in 1864. Both poets died in tragic circumstances; Shelley was drowned in a sailing accident, and Clare died in the Northampton General Lunatic Asylum where he had spent the last 23 years of his life. However, the poems printed here are very different – Shelley's poem is very still, whereas Clare's poem is full of life.

Ozymandias

I met a traveller from an antique land
Who said: Two vast and trunkless legs of stone
Stand in the desert … Near them, on the sand,
Half sunk, a shattered visage lies, whose frown,
And wrinkled lip, and sneer of cold command,
Tell that its sculptor well those passions read
Which yet survive, stamped on these lifeless things,
The hand that mocked them, and the heart that fed:
And on the pedestal these words appear:
'My name is Ozymandias, king of kings:
Look on my works, ye Mighty, and despair!'
Nothing beside remains. Round the decay
Of that colossal wreck, boundless and bare
The lone and level sands stretch far away.

P B Shelley (1792–1822)

(see Drama Approaches, page 158)

● ● ● ● ● ● ● ● ● ● ● ●

Looking closely

1   Use the following questions to help you to talk about the poem.
    Work with a partner or in a small group and make brief notes for
    each answer.

    a   What is written on the statue?
    b   Why do you imagine King Ozymandias ordered these words to be
        inscribed on his statue?
    c   When the statue was completed, what do you imagine the king
        was thinking as he looked at it?
    d   Ozymandias was a powerful ruler. The statue probably stood in
        the middle of a vast city. What is actually left of that city?
    e   What is left of the statue?
    f   Do you think that the sculptor *knew* that the statue would not
        last forever? Find a line in the poem to support your answer.
    g   What do the words in the poem 'decay' and 'wreck' describe?
        Where exactly in the poem do these words appear?
    h   The poet says 'Nothing beside remains'. But, what, exactly has
        survived in the sands? What do you think the poet is really
        trying to say?

Response

1   Imagine you have been transported one thousand years into the
    future. Think about an impressive building, statue or monument in
    your own town. Imagine that in one thousand years' time it has
    fallen into decay.

    a   Make notes of the words and phrases that you might use to
        describe your chosen building or monument. Then make notes of
        phrases to describe the immediate surroundings.
    b   Put your notes together to form a poem.

Signs of Winter (extract)

The cat runs races with her tail. The dog
Leaps o'er the orchard hedge and knarls* the grass.
The swine run round and grunt and play with straw,
Snatching out hasty mouthfuls from the stack.
Sudden upon the elm-tree tops the crows
Unceremonious visit pays and croaks,
Then swops away. From mossy barn the owl
Bobs hasty out – wheels round and, scared as soon,
As hastily retires. The ducks grow wild
And from the muddy pond fly up and wheel
A circle round the village and soon tired
Plunge in the pond again. The maids in haste
Snatch from the orchard hedge the mizled* clothes
And laughing hurry in to keep them dry.

JOHN CLARE (1793–1864)

* Knarles – nibbles   * mizled – wet with drizzle

Response

1   Some scenes in the poem could still occur in the countryside today; some scenes have disappeared forever. Discuss what this poem tells you about how the countryside has changed over the last 150 years.

2   Work in groups to create a still picture of the scene in 'Signs of Winter'. Each person in the group should take up a position that captures the energy of the poem.

Choose a short section from the poem to caption your still picture.

Comparing poems

1   a   In 'Ozymandias', Shelley uses many **adjectives** (words to describe).
Pick out all the adjectives, for example 'antique' land. What feeling or mood do these words create?

   b   In 'Signs of Winter' Clare uses many **verbs** (words for action).
Pick out all the verbs in this poem, for example 'The Cat *runs races*'. What feeling or mood do these words create?

Response

1 Write your own poem under one of the following titles:
Signs of Winter in Town
Signs of Spring in the Countryside

Use the following points to help you:
● Think about things you have actually observed in the town or
  countryside, for example, the steady beat of windscreen wipers in
  winter in town.
● What sort of mood do you want to create? You might think of
  town in winter as a place of bustle and movement or you might
  think of it as a place of weariness and boredom. You might think
  of spring in the countryside as a place of energy and life or as a
  place of peacefulness.
● When you have decided what sort of mood you want to create,
  think about the words and phrases you will choose to describe
  that mood. Think particularly about the adjectives and verbs you
  choose.

13 Isabella; or, The Pot of Basil

'Isabella; or, The Pot of Basil' was written by John Keats. John Keats was one of a group known as the Romantic Poets. He was born in 1795, and died from the disease, consumption, in 1821. Although he lived for only a short time, he wrote some of the finest poems to appear in the English language. 'Isabella' is not one of his great poems, but it is certainly interesting and memorable.

Isabella; or, The Pot of Basil

This is the story of two lovers, Lorenzo and Isabella, and of how they suffered for their love. It is a tale of greed, and betrayal, and ultimately, of murder and madness. But read on, and all will be revealed.

Isabella was the sister of two wealthy brothers who lived long ago in the city of Florence. These brothers were rich; they owned mines and factories and slaves. They loved money, and they were determined that their sister should make a good marriage to a wealthy lord. Imagine how they felt when they discovered that Isabella had been having secret meetings with Lorenzo, a poor young man.

A Story from Boccaccio

All close they met again, before the dusk
Had taken from the stars its pleasant veil,
All close they met, all eyes, before the dusk
Had taken from the stars its pleasant veil,
Close in a bower of hyacinth and musk,
Unknown of any, free from whispering tale.
Ah! better had it been for ever so,
Than idle ears should pleasure in their woe.

With her two brothers this fair lady dwelt,
Enriched from ancestral merchandize,
And for them many a weary hand did swelt
In torched mines and noisy factories,
And many once proud–quiver'd loins did melt
In blood from stinging whip; – with hollow eyes
Many all day in dazzling river stood,
To take the rich–ored driftings of the flood.

These brethren having found by many signs
What love Lorenzo for their sister had,
And how she lov'd him too, each unconfines
His bitter thoughts to other, well nigh mad
That he, the servant of their trade designs,
Should in their sister's love be blithe and glad,
When 'twas their plan to coax her by degrees
To some high noble and his olive–trees.

1 Role play

Work in pairs. You are Isabella's proud, greedy brothers. Act out the scene where you meet to discuss what to do about Isabella and Lorenzo. Think about where the scene is taking place. Remember, you are meeting secretly, so try to talk in a conspiratorial manner. After you have worked through the scene, take turns to share with your class the different decisions you have reached.

the poem continued ...

And Many a jealous conference had they,
And many times they bit their lips alone,
Before they fix'd upon a surest way
To make the youngster for his crime atone;
And at the last, these men of cruel clay
Cut Mercy with a sharp knife to the bone;
For they resolved in some forest dim
To kill Lorenzo, and there bury him.

There was Lorenzo slain and buried in,
There in that forest did his great love cease;
Ah! when a soul doth thus its freedom win,
It aches in loneliness – is ill at peace
As the break-covert blood-hounds of such sin:
They dipp'd their swords in the water, and did tease
Their horses homeward, with convulsed spur,
Each richer by his being a murderer.

2 Mime

Work in groups of three. As a mime, and in slow motion, show the murder of Lorenzo. Before beginning, re-read the second part in your groups. Decide exactly *how* the brothers killed Lorenzo, and how they got rid of any incriminating evidence.

the poem continued ...

They told their sister how, with sudden speed,
Lorenzo had ta'en ship for foreign lands,
Because of some great urgency and need
In their affairs, requiring trusty hands.
Poor Girl! put on thy stifling widow's weed,
And 'scape at once from Hope's accursed bands;
To-day thou wilt not see him, nor to-morrow,
And the next day will be a day of sorrow.

Well, as far as the brothers were concerned, that was the end of the affair. They had disposed of Lorenzo, hidden his corpse in the forest, told their sister that he had had to go abroad, and, hopefully, she would forget all about the wretched young man. But love will find a way. One night, at midnight, something woke Isabella from sleep, and there, at the foot of her bed, stood the ghost of Lorenzo.

● ● ● ● ● ● ● ● ● ● ● ●

It was a vision. – In the drowsy gloom,
The dull of midnight, at her couch's foot
Lorenzo stood, and wept: the forest tomb
Had Marr'd his glossy hair which once could shoot
Lustre into the sun, and put cold doom
Upon his lips, and taken the soft lute
From his lorn voice, and past his loamed ears
Had made a miry channel for his tears.

Saying moreover, "Isabel, my sweet!
"Red whortle-berries droop above my head,
"And a large flint-stone weighs upon my feet;
"Around me beeches and high chestnuts shed
"Their leaves and prickly nuts; A sheep-fold bleat
"Comes from beyond the river to my bed:
"Go, shed one tear upon my heather-bloom,
"And it shall comfort me within the tomb.

3 Freeze
Work in small groups. Show the ghost scene as a series of frozen
pictures. Now choose appropriate lines from the poem to caption
the pictures.

the poem continued ...

When the full morning came, she had devised
How she might secret to the forest hie;
How she might find the clay, so dearly prized,
And sing to it one latest lullaby;
How her short absence might be unsurmised,
While she the inmost of the dream would try.
Resolv'd she took with her an aged nurse,
And went into that dismal forest-hearse.

See, as they creep along the river side,
How she doth whisper to that aged Dame,
And, after looking round the champaign wide,
Shows her a knife. – "What feverous hectic flame
"Burns in thee, child? – What good can thee betide,
"That thou should'st smile again?" – The evening came,
And they had found Lorenzo's earthy bed;
The flint was there, the berries at his head.

*She cut off Lorenzo's head, washed it with her tears, combed its hair, wrapped
it in a silk scarf and then buried it in a pot of basil.*

In anxious secrecy they took it home,
And then the prize was all for Isabel:
She calm'd its wild hair with a golden comb,
And all around each eye's sepulchral cell
Pointed each fringed lash; the smeared loam
With tears, as chilly as a dripping well,
She drench'd away: – and still she comb'd, and kept
Sighing all day – and still she kiss'd, and wept.

Then in a silken scarf, – sweet with the dews
Of precious flowers pluck'd in Araby,
And divine liquids come with odorous ooze
Through the cold serpent-pipe refreshfully, –
She wrapp'd it up; and for its tomb did choose
A garden-pot, wherein she laid it by,
And cover'd it with mould, and o'er it set
Sweet Basil, which her tears kept ever wet.

● ● ● ● ● ● ● ● ● ● ● ●

And she forgot the stars, the moon, and sun,
And she forgot the blue above the trees,
And she forgot the dells where waters run,
And she forgot the chilly autumn breeze;
She had no knowledge when the day was done,
And the new morn she saw not: but in peace
Hung over her sweet Basil evermore,
And moisten'd it with tears unto the core.

Yet they contriv'd to steal the Basil-pot,
And to examine it in secret place;
The thing was vile with green and livid spot,
And yet they knew it was Lorenzo's face:
The guerdon of their murder they had got,
And so left Florence in a moment's space,
Never to turn again. – Away they went,
With blood upon their heads, to banishment.

And so she pined, and so she died forlorn,
Imploring for her Basil to the last.
No heart was there in Florence but did mourn
In pity of her love, so overcast.
And a sad ditty of this story born
From mouth to mouth through all the country pass'd:
Still is the burthen sung – "O cruelty,
"To steal my Basil-pot away from me!"

And so the story ends. Poor Isabella! After all that effort, to have the head
stolen from her by her brothers – no wonder the poor girl went mad and died.

4 Television documentary

You are going to work as a whole class producing a television documentary.

You are now in the present day. Imagine that the remains of the pot, containing a skull and remnants of a silk scarf, have been found. Decide where the pot was found, and under what circumstances, for example:

a The pot was found hidden under the floor of the old house whilst the house was being renovated.
or
b The house has been turned into a school, and the pot was discovered by some children exploring the grounds.

Form small groups of people involved in the discovery, for example, forensic experts, local historians, builders, descendants of the brothers and so on, and take turns to be interviewed on the programme.

Writing

Write a modern-day newspaper article on the discovery of the pot and its contents. Use the information revealed during the drama to help you with the writing.

Drama Approaches

This section offers extended drama activities for certain poems.

Gothic Poetry: 'The Witch' (page 18)

1 a **Role play**

   Sit in one circle. One person read aloud the first verse of
   'The Witch'.

   b In pairs improvise what happened in the *first* verse. Watch and
   discuss one or two interpretations of the poem.

   c Divide into pairs. **A** is the person inside the house, **B** is an
   interviewer. **B** must find out as much as possible about who the
   person outside was.

   ● Where did they come from?
   ● Did **A** let them in?
   ● Did they know each other?
   ● How long did the person stay?

   d Back in the circle, share information.

   e Every second person steps outside the circle. Half the class (outer
   circle) become homeless people. Half the class (inner circle)
   become the villagers. The homeless then persuade the villagers to
   let them in.

   f After this role play, the outsiders explain how they felt during the
   action.

   g Now read the whole poem, and discuss how the addition of the
   third verse changes your perception of the girl.

● ● ● ● ● ● ● ● ● ● ●

Dragon Days: 'Atmosfear' (page 41)

1 **Discussion**

Sit in a circle and read the poem 'Atmosfear' aloud. Discuss immediate responses to the poem:
- what did you imagine as the poem was read?
- are there any words or phrases you particularly enjoyed?

2 **Role play**

One person (possibly teacher) narrates:

It is the year 2004. In the far wastelands of the North Pole, a local hunting party noticed deep cracks that have appeared in the ice, and heard mysterious grinding noises. You are the scientists who have been called in to investigate.

Working in small groups, act out the arrival of the scientists, and their preliminary investigations. The nature of this investigation is cautious – the scientists may have their suspicions about what is happening, and may find certain clues, but nothing conclusive.

3 **Telephone conversations**

Work in pairs – join with someone from a different group. Sitting back-to-back, report and discuss your findings as a telephone conversation. At a signal from your teacher, listen in to snatches of conversation from other pairs.

4 **Group improvisations**

One person (possibly teacher) narrates:

While the scientists were working at the North Pole, an important break-through in Time Travel had been made in a university in Britain.

This enabled small groups to travel back to a point in time of their choice, and to remain there for a maximum of ten minutes.

a   Keep in small groups of four or five. Half the class goes back in time to the 1990s. Some of you should keep in roles as scientists from the future, others should adopt roles as scientists from the '90s. Act out a meeting between these two groups.
   ● What will they want to say to each other and ask each other?
   ● How can they help each other?

b   The rest of the class remains as groups of scientists working at the North Pole. Each group now makes a new discovery.
   (Re-read the poem to give you more ideas.)

5   Edited highlights

Each group has made a video of their experiences. The scientists are preparing to 'edit' the 'videos' to a maximum of three minutes each.

Decide which parts of your work from (4) to show. Work on these moments for presentation, and then share them with the rest of your class. One person from each group may become the link person explaining what is about to be shown in the video.

6   Ideas round-up

Re-assemble in a circle. Read the poem once more and give your final reactions.

Acknowledgement:- Jonathan Neelands – *Learning through Imagined Experience.*
Hodder & Stoughton
(The poem and a similar idea for drama is presented)

● ● ● ● ● ● ● ● ● ● ● ●

War: 'Death of an Aircraft' (page 59)

This drama should be worked through *before* the poem is read.

1 Role play
Teacher in role of German officer in Second World War in Crete narrates:

An aeroplane has crashed on the beach.

Seven of you play the roles of German soldiers guarding the plane.

a Three others chosen secretly by your teacher will become resistance fighters. You will be able to watch and listen to what is going on in the rest of the drama. The rest become villagers.

b The villagers try to persuade the soldiers to leave the aeroplane. You must think of good reasons to lure away the soldiers. At an appropriate moment, perhaps as the rest of the class is frozen, the three resistance fighters set fire to the aeroplane.

c Teacher in role as furious German officer: (to soldiers) *I order you to round-up the villagers now.* (then to villagers) *The resistance fighters must surrender or your whole village will be shot.* Villagers must make a decision.

2 Now read the poem and compare the ending with the outcome of the drama.

Return to the Sea: 'Song of the Sea and People' (page 85)

1   You are going to work as a whole class to create an impression of a storm at sea.

a   Work on your own. Look back over *all* the poems in **Return to the Sea**, and choose a couple of lines from one poem to learn by heart. Choose exciting lines that capture the dangerous nature of the sea.

b   When you have learnt your lines, decide for yourself how you are going to say them; will they be whispered, shouted, hissed, etc?

c   As a class, take turns to speak your lines. Gradually increase the pace of the words to give the effect of a turbulent storm. Add a simple movement of your own, for example, a twist of your body. Put the words and movements together.

2   **Forum theatre**

a   As a class, sit in a circle with a large space in the centre and read 'Song of the Sea and People'.

b   Re-read the first verse. Volunteers step into the circle to make a frozen picture depicting the events of that verse. The audience make suggestions for alterations to the picture, and physically manipulate the 'actors' to make a satisfactory interpretation of the verse. Relax the picture.

c   Read the second verse. The audience adjust the picture to depict the events.

d   Repeat for the third verse. Each time, the adjustments will probably only be small, but vital to the meaning of the poem. The audience should concentrate on getting the right expressions on the actors' faces.

e   Finally, re-read the whole poem with the picture changing as you read from first to second to third verse.

● ● ● ● ● ● ● ● ● ● ● ●

Heroes for All Time: 'Sir Gawain and the Green Knight'
(page 123)

The poem should not be read until after the first four drama activities.

1 Statue

Six of you should be positioned as follows:

- King Arthur and Queen Guinevere seated.
- Two servants to stand either side of king and queen with hands positioned as if holding platters etc.
- Kneeling in front of the king and queen, the Green Knight. His head should be bent forward as if about to receive a blow on the neck.
- Sir Gawain, hands raised aloft as if to strike with an axe.

When the statue has been created, remain in position while the rest of the class studies what has been made. Discuss what is going on and who these people might be.

2 Role play

Exploring a story leading up to this dramatic moment.
The story is set in medieval times, in the days of King Arthur and Queen Guinevere. It is late in December when there is much feasting and merry-making to celebrate the time of Christmas. King and queen should remain in position. One by one, knights, ladies and servants state their role in the banquet scene, and take up their position, eg
'I am a young serving girl, and I am about to offer my Lord some fruit.'
When everyone is in position, the drama begins.

3 Thought tracking

Green Knight (as before) enters the banquet scene and freezes action. The Green Knight tells the merry-makers who he is and issues the challenge. Green Knight will allow any person to deal him one blow with his axe, on condition that that same person agrees to meet him a year hence at the Green Chapel where he will receive the return blow.

Teacher asks what each person is thinking at this point. Everyone should speak in role.

4 Group discussion

    a In small groups talk together about what has happened and what the knights, ladies and servants should do.

It is revealed that one knight, Sir Gawain, accepts the challenge.

    b Read the poem.

5 Freeze

Back in role, show what happens in the poem as three frozen moments in time. Each frozen moment should be given a caption.

12 Two Scenes in Time: 'Ozymandias' (page 138)

Using a large piece of rectangular card make an ancient stone tablet inscribed with the words of the poem.

a Improvisation

You are all archaeologists working together to explore an historical site in Egypt. After an appropriate time working at the site you discover the stone tablet. Read the words inscribed on the tablet, and discuss what they could mean.

b Role-play

Next you will all travel back in time, thousands of years to the reign of Ozymandias when a huge monument is being erected to celebrate the rule of the great king. Choose a role to adopt: slave or overseer, stomemason or sculptor, member of the royal family or just an interested passer-by and take turns to speak your thoughts.

c Slow-motion mime

The drama moves on several centuries. The great city has crumbled into dust, and all that remains is the huge stone memorial to Ozymandias. In groups, freeze into position to make sections of that memorial. At a given signal, a crack appears and in slow-motion, the memorial splits apart to become nothing more than rubble.

Glossary

Adjectives Words which give more information about, or modify, nouns, *e.g., my black cat.*

Alliteration This is the name given to the repeated use of the same sound at the beginning of two or more words that are close to each other. It helps the poet to create an effective sound, to emphasize certain words or to reinforce meaning, *e.g., the western wind was wild.*

Ballad A story told in regular, rhyming, rhythmic stanzas. The first ballads were folk-poems, meant to be sung with musical accompaniment. Ballads are simple, dramatic tales of events in human life and often have a chorus for communal presentation and participation.

Compound words A word made up of two or more words, *e.g., tea pot.*

Imagery The way writers use language to create an imagined picture or feeling in a reader's mind. An image will appeal directly to one or more of the five senses – sight, sound, taste or smell. *E.g., the yellow leaves flickered and rustled like burning newspapers.*

Onomatopoeic Words which are used to form the word they are describing, so that sound and sense echo each other, *e.g.,* the *buzz* of a bee.

Parody A humorous or mocking imitation of the style of a writer or speaker. Often typical features of the style are exaggerated in order to make a point or to exploit a weakness.

Personification Referring to a thing or an idea as if it were a person.

Refrain A single phrase which is repeated throughout a poem.

Rhyming couplets A rhyming couplet is a pair of lines that rhyme. It is possible for a whole poem to be made up of couplets. 'Sir Eglamour' is an example of such a poem.

Thesaurus A resource (it can be a book or computer program) which contains lists of words which mean the same thing.

Verbs Words which describe action, e.g., *throwing* a ball.

Index